"Honest, cogent, practical, and deep, *Outsmart Your Smartphone* addresses an issue at the forefront of nearly every parent's and every young adult's worry list—that is, has my smartphone outsmarted me? Through a step-by-step, sensitive, evidence-based approach, Davis challenges the reader by suggesting do-able strategies to enhance real connections, foster positive life skills, and reduce undue reliance on those rectangular, 'intelligent' objects that dominate our lives. Highly recommended."

—**Stephen Hinshaw, PhD**, professor in the department of psychology at the University of California, Berkeley; professor in the department of psychiatry at the University of California, San Francisco; and author of *Another Kind of Madness*

"Our smartphones are making us miserable, yet we increasingly need them to navigate our lives. How can we prioritize happiness, balance, and connection, despite this tech? That's where happiness psychologist and researcher Tchiki Davis comes in. She shares seven game-changing steps we can take to lead happier lives with our smartphones. Through stories of her own and others' experiences, along with insights from brain science and behavioral research, Tchiki empowers us to build a healthier relationship with our smartphone."

—**Gayle Allen, EdD, MBA**, CEO of The Innovators' Circle, and host of the *Curious Minds* podcast

"Put down your smartphone, and pick up this book! Masterfully written, this guide by Tchiki Davis is truly a gem! This is the first book in the happiness domain I've read that actually provides real and practical skills you can implement into your life this instant. In addition to the outstanding research and empirically driven ideas this book offers, Davis has a voice that is witty, highly relatable, and deeply empathic. She is the perfect coach to help any of us overcome our smartphone addictions, and becoming a more well-balanced and happier individual. Thank you, Tchiki Davis!"

> —**Goali Saedi Bocci, PhD**, adjunct professor at
> Pepperdine's graduate school of education and psychology;
> and author of *The Social Media Workbook for Teens* and
> the *Digital Detox Card Deck*

"This book applies nuggets of wisdom and much of the self-help literature to a modern problem that affects almost all of us. If you want to own your smartphone instead of it owning you, reading *Outsmart Your Smartphone* is a great place to start!"

> —**Stephen M. Kosslyn, PhD**, president and CEO of
> Foundry College

"It will take an army to conquer technology abuse. In her new book, Tchiki Davis proves herself as a worthy captain of the cause. Well researched, prescriptive, and practical, *Outsmart Your Smartphone* is not only good medicine, it's a good read."

> —**Blake Snow**, online journalist, off-line advocate, and
> author of *Log Off*

"This actionable, easy-to-understand guide gives you the tools you need to get back in charge of a tool that's taken over many of our lives: our mobile phones. Read it and you'll have a clear path to reclaiming time that slips away, redirecting yourself toward what matters, and setting a good example for all of those people around you who are also drawn more and more into their mobile phones. Read it!"

—**Ellen Petry Leanse**, best-selling author of
The Happiness Hack, and chief people officer at Lucidworks

"Tchiki Davis tackles the complex relationship between our smartphones and being happy. With solid research, crisp advice, and personal stories, *Outsmart Your Smartphone* goes beyond the standard self-help patter to provide a thoughtful guide to living with your smartphone in a way that doesn't make you unhappy or crazy."

—**Victor J. Strecher, PhD, MPH**, professor at the
University of Michigan School of Public Health

"Many of us have the sinking feeling that modern technologies are undermining our relationships, our focus, and, ultimately, our happiness. But Tchiki Davis shows us that it doesn't have to be that way. With great candor and insight, she deftly walks us through sensible, research-based steps to reclaim our sense of purpose and equanimity in the digital age. *Outsmart Your Smartphone* will help you realize that you're not alone in your struggles with technology—and gently guide you toward healthier relationships with your devices, with other people, and with yourself."

—**Jason Marsh**, editor in chief and director of programs
at the Greater Good Science Center at the University of
California, Berkeley

"What if technology could support, rather than undermine, our health and well-being? In this well-researched, honest, and accessible guide, Tchiki Davis pulls together the best evidence from the field of positive psychology about the real drivers of human happiness—living with purpose, kindness to others, meaningful social connection—and shares simple actions you can take today to take back your attention, live with intention, and get technology on your side. For anyone who's ever thought, *I'll just quickly check my phone*, and lost an hour (or more!), this book is for us."

—**Jana Haritatos, PhD**, vice president of research
at Hopelab Foundation

OUTSMART
YOUR
SMARTPHONE

CONSCIOUS TECH HABITS
for FINDING HAPPINESS,
BALANCE & CONNECTION IRL

Tchiki Davis, PhD

New Harbinger Publications, Inc.

Publisher's Note

This publication is designed to provide accurate and authoritative information in regard to the subject matter covered. It is sold with the understanding that the publisher is not engaged in rendering psychological, financial, legal, or other professional services. If expert assistance or counseling is needed, the services of a competent professional should be sought.

Distributed in Canada by Raincoast Books

Copyright © 2019 by Tchiki Davis

New Harbinger Publications, Inc.
5674 Shattuck Avenue
Oakland, CA 94609
www.newharbinger.com

Cover design by Sara Christian

Acquired by Ryan Buresh

Edited by Gretel Hakanson

All Rights Reserved

FSC
www.fsc.org
MIX
Paper from
responsible sources
FSC® C011935

Library of Congress Cataloging-in-Publication Data on file

Printed in the United States of America

21   20   19

10   9   8   7   6   5   4   3   2   1   First Printing

For you, my readers.

Contents

Foreword

I first started following Doctor Tchiki Davis as a fellow blogger for *Psychology Today*. Her articles drew me in with their clarity, vulnerability, expert knowledge, and on-trend focus. Davis is a Bay Area resident who works closely with Silicon Valley to integrate her knowledge about the science of happiness with cutting edge technology products and research. Psychologists today can use the internet and smartphones to spread their research knowledge and tools to a broad, international audience, Davis is a fresh and innovative voice for our information age.

In her new book *Outsmart Your Smartphone*, Davis skillfully tackles the topic of how technology impacts our happiness, and she offers a clear, practical, and research-based approach to gaining control over technology so you can live a happier, balanced, more socially connected, and purposeful life. While many books have been written on the science of happiness, few offer an individualized, tech-savvy approach to finding happiness in an era of ever-present technology. This book fills an important gap because it makes happiness knowledge more accessible to a younger generation in the age of smartphones.

Davis begins with the premise that we are all becoming less happy despite an increase in per capita income. She offers a thoughtful, convincing analysis of how technology diminishes our happiness by changing the nature of work, decreasing opportunities for meaningful social connection, hijacking our attention away from the present moment, and creating manufactured images of beauty and success that give us FOMO (fear of missing out), which makes our lives seem dull and insufficient by comparison. She then offers a seven-step solution for engaging more mindfully with technology, setting boundaries with our smartphones, and using technology to serve our most authentic needs, values, and goals. Davis's prescriptions integrate many of the traditional tenets of happiness research including mindfulness, resilience, gratitude, compassion, growth mindset, habit change, and service to others.

What is unique about this book is the application of this knowledge in an immensely practical way to our daily interactions with technology. *Outsmarting Your Smartphone* provides a roadmap to lasting happiness that emphasizes relatedness, purpose, authentic self-expression, a balanced life, and autonomy. The book then proceeds to explain how technology and smartphone use can get in the way, distracting us from the parts of life that matter most when it comes to our long-term happiness. What follows is a clear and clever prescription for controlling our smartphone use, rather than letting our smartphones control us. Davis intersperses poignant anecdotes from her own life that illustrate both our human fallibility and misdirection as well as how we can, in fact, build a happier life with the help of expert knowledge, repeated practice, a growth mindset, and self-compassion.

At the end of the book she outlines a vision of what the world might look like if individuals, tech companies, communities, and societies made happiness a top priority. By following the pathways suggested in this book, you will be well on your way to building the components of a happy and authentic life that involve focusing compassionately outside of yourself as well as within.

—Melanie Greenberg, Ph.D.
Clinical Psychologist, Life and Business Coach,
International Speaker, Media Expert, Blogger,
and Author of *The Stress-Proof Brain* and *The Mindful Self-Express* blog on *Psychology Today*.

Introduction

I was fifteen. It was a Halloween night, and my friend's parents were out of town. So don't tell my mom, but I went to a party.

Late in the night, the house was still filled with the sounds of teenagers, laughing inanely about whatever we thought was funny back then. At some point, I wandered into the kitchen to get a drink of water. There, standing alone, was a friend of mine. Her head was cast downward, her bangs were in front of her eyes, and she was squeezing her hand into a tight fist. As I walked up to her, I saw something red on her hand. It was blood!

I rushed over to her, grabbing her hand, demanding that she let me help her. But she jerked away from me, hiding her hand. Tears started flooding her eyes.

Finally, after much prodding, she opened her hand. Lying in her palm was a piece of glass, glass that she had been squeezing as hard as she possibly could. She was so upset about something—I still don't know what it was to this day—that she pushed that piece of glass against her skin until blood was literally dripping on the floor.

I didn't know it at the time, but that moment was the first in a series of moments that would change my life. In the years that followed, I saw the scars from self-harm, I saw the glazed-over eyes that come with drug abuse, and I saw the skin that hangs off a body that is being intentionally starved. I witnessed the depths of depression and the heights of mania, suicide attempts and near overdoses. The world I lived in seemed to be a really unhappy place.

It turns out that a person can only see so much human suffering before becoming determined to stop it—or at least that's what happened to me. Somewhere along the way, my life's mission became to help people manage negative emotions, cope in healthier ways, and build the skills that would help them feel a bit happier.

Still a fifteen-year-old, I started pursuing this mission by organizing drug-free social events for teens in my town. I continued working with at-risk youth all through college and in the years after graduating. Then, I got into grad school—I hoped to finally learn the science of happiness and be able to make a bigger impact in the lives of the people I worked with.

After finishing my master's degree, I got into UC Berkeley, which housed one of the best psychology programs in the world. While completing my PhD, I continued pursuing my mission, learning everything I could about emotions, happiness, and well-being. I then used these insights to create "tech-based solutions for unhappiness"—apps, courses, and other online tools designed to help people build their happiness. I even won a few awards for these innovations. After graduating, I continued creating tech-based solutions for unhappiness—these solutions have now reached more than a million people worldwide.

Perhaps this might have been the end of a wonderful success story. But that's not how it felt to me, not at all. Remember my mission to help people increase their happiness? Well, I felt like I was failing miserably. In fact, the more I became an expert at the intersection of happiness and technology, the more I started to see *a giant problem*—a problem that was preventing most people from increasing their happiness, no matter what they did, no matter how hard they tried. This problem was "smartphone syndrome."

In our technology-obsessed world, we now rely on our smartphones and other devices for work, information, or simply calling for a lift. As a result, we have developed a new set of emotional and behavioral patterns—patterns that make us feel unhappy, unbalanced, and unconnected. But because of our 24-7 access to the Internet, media, and social media, we never have the opportunity to step back and see how technology is *really* affecting us. And even if we *knew* how technology was affecting us, it's not like we could just quit because we're both reliant on technology for our livelihood and addicted to the spurts of happiness that our devices provide. So we're in a predicament where our devices are ruining our happiness, yet we can't stop using them.

So what *can* we do? How do we outsmart our smartphones? To succeed in my mission to increase happiness, I knew I needed to answer this question. And as an expert smack-dab in the middle of the happiness and technology industries, I knew I was the right person for the job. So I started researching, testing, and reflecting on the different strategies we can use to outsmart our smartphones. And that's how this book was born.

In this book, you'll discover seven steps the will help you outsmart your smartphone. When you take these steps, you'll learn how to use technology in healthier ways. You'll discover how to limit your use of technology in the ways that promote happiness. And you'll start to find happiness, balance, and true connection in spite of using technology.

As you progress through the seven steps, you'll have me there with you, sharing my personal successes and failures, easy wins and tough challenges, and epiphanies and slow painful growth as I too work on outsmarting *my* smartphone and building happiness in this screen-obsessed world. By the end of the book, you'll understand why it seems so much harder to find happiness now, in the technology age. But you'll also be equipped with new skills that will help you meet these new challenges. And you won't even have to throw out your phone!

WHAT IS HAPPINESS ANYWAY?

One day, right around my twenty-first birthday, my eyes hungrily searched through my knickknacks and cherished items, looking for just the right thing to chuck across the room. Aha! I reached for a vase my partner had given me. Suddenly, my arm pitched it across the room, shattering it against the wall, raining tiny shards of glass onto the carpet. I immediately regretted it, quickly realizing that this was a really stupid way to express my emotions.

I didn't *want* to act like this. But for some reason, I did it anyway. Some part of me chose to feel this way, to think this way, and to act this way.

It all started in my childhood (don't worry, I'm not going to get all Sigmund Freud-y on you because it's actually a lot simpler than all that). My mom raised me, mostly on her own, so she was busy and distracted. Over time, I learned that if I wanted to get her attention, all I had to do was throw a tantrum. So I did it…again and again. And it worked, again and again.

Tantrums worked so well for me that at some point, I started throwing them to get what I wanted from my friends…and that often worked too. I didn't know at the time that what I was doing was immature, obnoxious, and a piss-poor way to get what I wanted. All I knew was that tantrums helped me get my needs met. So they were actually really *helpful* for me for a long time.

But now I was an adult. I didn't want to act like this anymore. I could see how my tantrums were making everyone, including me, miserable. But I didn't know how to stop. This behavior had become as automatic as breathing, and the idea of not having a tantrum when I "needed" one felt like drowning. How had I gotten stuck using this horrible coping strategy? And why was it so hard to stop, even when I really wanted to?

Well, it turns out that it was my stupid brain's fault. In childhood, our brains pay attention to every situation we're in and how we respond. If we do something and get a positive response, our brain counts that as a win. So it makes it easier to do that same thing again next time, and it's even easier the time after that, and so on. Our brains do this because they are trying to make life easier for us by automating the things we do a lot. This is usually a good thing because if our brains had to expend effort on every…tiny…little…thing, we'd be paralyzed by it. But, it also means that we can get *stuck* feeling the emotions we have always felt, thinking the way we have always thought, and acting the way we have always acted…even if it's not making us happy anymore.

And my silly brain? Well, it automated temper tantrums. I didn't know what to do instead, so I kept having tantrums, which unintentionally trained my brain to keep having them. So the more times I threw a tantrum, the harder it was to change. And as hard as it is to admit, yes, I was still throwing tantrums in my twenties.

Embarrassing? Absolutely. But I'm telling you this story because I know your brain is stuck doing stupid things too. We all have problematic habits hardwired in our brains. Maybe *you* don't throw tantrums— I hope for your sake that you don't. But I know that you too have hardwired habits that you want to change…otherwise you wouldn't be here with me. The truth is, we all get stuck thinking, feeling, and behaving in ways that don't make us happy. And regardless of what our particular challenge is, the same approach can be used to overcome it.

The bad news is that the longer you've been doing anything— whether it be throwing tantrums, smoking cigarettes, or even using your smartphone in unhealthy ways, the harder it will be to change— to retrain your brain. It will require you to feel, think, and act in totally new ways—ways that feel uncomfortable at times and downright awful other times. And you'll have to continue to feel this discomfort for long enough that your brain starts to automate new patterns, the types of patterns that help you outsmart your smartphone and finally find happiness, balance, and true connection in this technology-crazed world.

The good news is that your lazy brain hates extra work, so it really *wants* to automate these new, healthier patterns as quickly as possible. That means that the hardest part is getting started. And the longer you stick to using the skills in this book, the easier they will get. And you know the truly amazing part? If you work at it—I mean *really* work at it—your brain will eventually automate the thoughts, emotions, and behaviors that make you truly happy. In time, you'll manage your technology with ease, maintain healthy balance, and even experience true connection again…with hardly any effort at all.

You know how I know this works? Because I've done it! Most importantly, I am now completely tantrum-free. But in the years since discovering this method, I've continued using it, building one positive skill at a time and helping others do the same. So by the time I realized that our smartphones were hurting our happiness, I was confident that this approach could help us overcome this challenge. It was just a matter of figuring out which thoughts, emotions, and behaviors we needed to change to outsmart our smartphones.

HOW TO BUILD "HAPPINESS SKILLS"

Anytime we want to increase happiness, balance, connection, or other types of mental wellness, we must build a particular set of skills—skills like mindfulness, positive thinking, kindness, and so forth. Building these "happiness skills" is the key to thinking, feeling, and acting in ways that make you happy. Unfortunately, now in the technology age, simply learning a random collection of these skills often *doesn't* lead to ongoing, long-term happiness for many people. Why? One reason is that building happiness skills is about so much more than what you do—it's about *how* you do it. Let me show you what I mean.

If you were just starting to learn math, what would you do? Well, you could first try some long division, then try some addition, and then find the circumference of a circle. But would this be the best way to learn math? Might it be better to start with specific skills, build on them, and slowly increase in difficulty as you become more skilled? The answer is obvious—it's really important that we follow the right steps in the right order. And that's true for more than just math; it's true when it comes to building happiness too.

So what are the right steps to take for happiness? Well, it depends on what personal challenges *you* face, what situations *you're* in, and what's happening in the world around *you*. That's why we need to look inward, to gain clarity on our personal challenges, *as well as* outward, to gain clarity on the social or cultural challenges we are *all* dealing with as a result of living in the technology age.

When we look inward, we can more easily identify the specific skills that we personally would benefit from most—for example, maybe we struggle with self-compassion, resilience, or living our purpose. And when we look outward, we can more easily identify the specific skills that nearly *everyone* struggles with in the technology age—for example most of us are now struggling with finding balance, staying mindful, and developing meaningful connections. When we focus on building these essential skills we can more quickly, easily, and effectively boost our happiness, even in the presence of modern technology.

BUILDING HAPPINESS IN THE TECHNOLOGY AGE

Some people say that modern technologies—TV, the Internet, and smartphones—are to blame for our all of our woes. There is some truth to this—modern technology is indeed having negative impacts on aspects of our happiness. But this nihilistic attitude does nothing to help us to fix the very real problem we have: our smartphones make it harder to be happy, but we can't live without them. What we really want to know is how to maintain our happiness *in spite* of our phones.

Luckily, technology is just a thing—plastic and metal and who knows what else all put together. It *can* be bad for us—for example, when smartphone notifications distract us from paying attention to the people we care about, when late-night surfing keeps us from getting restful sleep, or when artificial intelligence automates our jobs. But, technology can also be good for us—for example, when we text a friend to get support, when websites enable us to discover things that bring us joy, or when apps help us build happiness skills more easily. So technology, itself, is neither inherently bad nor inherently good for our happiness.

Technology is only bad for our happiness when it interferes with our happiness skills—remember, having strong happiness skills is the key to happiness. But not all technologies interfere with our happiness skills—we don't worry about our lawnmower, toaster, or teapot hurting our happiness, right? We only worry about certain modern technologies: our smartphones, the Internet, and social media. While it's true that these technologies *can* create unhealthy beliefs, an unbalanced lifestyle, or diminished social relationships, they *also* can provide support, inspiration, and opportunities for social connection. So we don't need to break up with our phones; we need to build a healthy relationship with our phones.

So how can we build a better relationship with our phones and other devices? By following seven key steps.

THE SEVEN STEPS

After years of research, hundreds of discussions, and a good amount of personal experimentation, I have come to believe that these seven steps are the key to finally finding happiness, balance, and true connection in our tech-obsessed world.

Step One: Build Foundational Skills

In this step, we'll go through how to set up systems for success, develop a growth mindset, and find balance. First, just as having a map can get you where you're going more quickly or having a recipe can help you make a tastier meal, setting up systems is key to making progress with your happiness. Second, growth mindset—or the belief that you actually can improve yourself—is key because if you don't *believe* you can outsmart your smartphone, it'll be really hard to do it. Third, balance is key because without it, you'll have less mental and physical energy to devote to creating a healthier relationship with your smartphone. Learning these foundational skills will help you start your happiness journey on the right foot.

Step Two: Stay Present

In this step, you'll discover how to stay mindful, sharpen your senses, and draw your attention to what's happening all around you. You'll learn how to deal with your fear of missing out, you'll discover how to create mindful moments, and you'll challenge yourself to take small but intentional breaks from technology—breaks that help you gain clarity about what you're *really* missing when you give all your attention to technology.

Step Three: Make Meaningful Connections

In this step, you'll learn how to create more meaningful social connections both on- and offline by strengthening relationships, focusing on others, and communicating kindly. These skills help you forge stronger bonds in your real life and your virtual life. It is these bonds that carry you through the good and the bad, helping you create a more durable form of happiness that's not as easily hurt by your smartphone.

Step Four: Manage Your Emotions

We ramp up in this step by discussing three emotional skills that are strongly linked to happiness in the technology age: self-compassion, positivity, and resilience. Building these skills helps you overcome some of the most common causes of unhappiness in the technology age: feeling bad about yourself, feeling bad about your life, and feeling bad about the things that happen to you.

Step Five: Practice Kindness

In this step, you'll discover how to use technology to practice kindness—the type of kindness that feels really good and makes you happy. You'll do this by exploring your values, finding your purpose, and applying these insights to make positive impacts IRL and online. As a result of these efforts, you can more easily turn away from technology and better focus on what really brings meaning into your life.

Step Six: Be True to Yourself

In this step, you'll work on a set of some of the more challenging skills to build in the technology age—skills like being yourself, speaking up for yourself, and opening yourself up to others. These skills tend to be harder because they require that you risk being judged, rejected, or even abandoned by others, an experience that is especially painful (and public) in the technology age. Although building these skills can be scary and even cause you pain in the short term, what emerges in the long term is a sense of true acceptance of yourself and others. Finally you can live your life, authentically, on your own terms.

Step Seven: Beat the Hedonic Treadmill

In this chapter, we'll talk about how to beat the hedonic treadmill—or the tendency for us to slowly slide back to our original level of happiness. You'll work on beating the hedonic treadmill by pursuing happiness in more social ways, getting out of your comfort zone, and making happiness a part of your daily routine. By implementing these strategies, you'll set yourself up for continued happiness—happiness that will persist long after you've finished this book. As a result, the journey we've taken here together won't be forgotten; it'll be integrated into your life in ways that benefit you permanently.

GETTING READY TO TAKE THE SEVEN STEPS

Are you ready to outsmart your smartphone? Great! Let's make sure you have everything you need to be successful.

First, you'll need a notebook or journal. You'll use this notebook to write your responses to questions, engage in thought experiments, and do activities that help you develop a healthier relationship with technology. Because these types of activities really help your brain turn *information* about happiness skills into the actual *skills* you need to increase happiness, I strongly recommend you do these activities to increase your happiness more quickly, easily, and effectively (Layous and Lyubomirsky 2012).

When choosing a notebook, be sure to choose something that works *for you*. You could use the notes app on your phone, download a journaling app, create a document on your computer, use a paper notebook, or grab the Outsmart Your Smartphone notebook from my website, http://www.berkeleywellbeing.com. The main objective here is to make it as easy as possible for you to build your happiness skills. So whatever notebook you choose, just be sure it fits into *your* lifestyle.

Right now, before continuing, take a moment to decide which notebook or app you'll use to complete the activities in this book. Once you have your notebook, keep it in a place that's easy to find. For example, if you downloaded an app, keep it on the first screen of your phone. If you started a document on your laptop, keep a link to it on your desktop. And if you have a paper notebook, keep it on your desk, in a bag you always have with you, or in another place where you'll see it regularly.

Next, decide which motivation boosters you'll use to stay on track with the seven steps. Because most of us find it hard to stick to our goals, we often need to use motivation boosters to achieve the *real* positive changes we desire. Which motivation boosters are a good fit *for you?* Let's find out.

Ask yourself, "Are you the kind of person who starts something new then quickly loses interest?" If so, I recommend you download the "28 Day Challenge to Outsmart Your Smartphone" instruction sheet. By doing the challenge, you'll have a reason to stay motivated for at least twenty-eight days. To start this challenge, go to the page for this book at http://www.newharbinger.com/43492 to get the challenge and other free resources. Feel free to share the challenge with your friends, family, and community if you think it would help you feel more motivated.

Now ask yourself, "Are you the kind of person who is more likely to do something when you have a friend to do it with?" If so, I suggest you consider buying a copy of this book for a buddy. You and your buddy can then do the seven steps together, share your experiences with one another, and hold each other accountable.

Or, if you prefer the support of virtual friends, you can search for the #OutsmartYourSmartphone hashtag on your favorite social media platform to start or join a conversation. You may also want to join or create an online group to provide a designated digital space for outsmarting your smartphone.

Lastly, ask yourself, "Are you the kind of person who tends to be more successful achieving your goals when you have structure or a schedule?" If so, consider creating a weekly Outsmart Your Smartphone activity group, Meetup, or gathering. Invite friends, family, coworkers, or people in your community to get together IRL once per week for at least seven weeks (one week per step). Use this time to talk about what you did that week to outsmart your smartphone, what gave you the most trouble, and how you could better manage this challenge in the future. Having this scheduled social time to work on outsmarting your smartphone is almost guaranteed to help you make faster progress because it provides added structure, social connection, and perspective sharing. For more ideas about what to include in your Outsmart Your Smartphone activity group, check out http://www.berkeleywell being.com. Although these motivation boosters generally contribute to easier, faster, and more efficient progress, it's entirely up to you to decide if any of these motivation boosters are a good fit *for you.*

Once you have chosen your notebook and your motivation boosters, you're all set to outsmart your smartphone and start the seven steps to finding happiness, balance, and true connection. I'm so glad you've decided to build a better relationship with technology, and I look forward to being your guide.

MEASURE YOUR STARTING POINT

When you are ready to start, the first thing to do is measure your starting point. You have scales to tell you if you are overweight, and you have exams to tell you which math skills to study more, but how do you know which skills you most need to outsmart your smartphone and build your happiness? You can find out by taking the Outsmart

Your Smartphone quiz. This quiz will give you a sense of your key trouble spots. And later, we'll use the quiz again to measure your progress. You can also download a copy of the quiz at http://www.newhar binger.com/43492.

Outsmart Your Smartphone Quiz

The purpose of this quiz is to help you identify which of the skills in this book will be most useful to *you* in outsmarting your smartphone. Please rate the following statements honestly using a scale of 1 to 10, where 1 means strongly disagree (that's not me at all) and 10 means strongly agree (that's me!).

Strongly disagree   Strongly agree

1   2   3   4   5   6   7   8   9   10

Step One: Build Foundational Skills

Skill	Statement	Rating
Growth Mindset	I'm unable to improve my relationship with my phone.	
Balance	I use my phone during times I have set aside to relax.	
Supportive Systems	I rarely use my phone in ways that help me reach my goals.	

Step Two: Stay Present

Skill	Statement	Rating
Fear of Missing Out	I feel anxious when I don't have my phone nearby.	
Technology Timeouts	I have a hard time taking breaks from my phone or the Internet.	
Mindful Moments	I pull out my phone during many of my spare moments.	

Step Three: Make Meaningful Connections

Skill	Statement	Rating
Strong Relationships	I check my phone while spending time with friends or family.	
Focus on Others	I focus mostly on myself (my pictures, posts, and pages) when I'm online.	
Communicate Kindly	I sometimes say mean things in messages, posts, or responses.	

Step Four: Manage Your Emotions

Skill	Statement	Rating
Self-Compassion	I feel bad about myself either in real life or online.	
Positivity	I have a hard time thinking positively about my life.	
Resilience	I struggle to recover from challenges, obstacles, or upsetting experiences.	

Step Five: Practice Kindness

Skill	Statement	Rating
Live Your Values	I struggle to understand or live my values.	
Find Your Purpose	I'm not sure what gives my life meaning or purpose.	
Make Positive Impacts	I rarely help others in ways that make me feel good.	

Step Six: Be True to Yourself

Skill	Statement	Rating
Be Yourself	*It's hard for me to show my faults, fears, and insecurities either online or offline.*	
Speak Up for Yourself	*I struggle to tell others what I need from them to be happy.*	
Open Yourself to Others	*I have a hard time accepting people who are different from me.*	

Step Seven: Beat the Hedonic Treadmill

Skill	Statement	Rating
Build Happiness with Others	*Anytime I pursue happiness, I do so alone, online, or on my phone.*	
Get Out of Your Comfort Zone	*I rarely try new things or get out of my comfort zone.*	
Make Happiness a Part of Your Daily Routine	*I have not really made happiness a priority in my life.*	

HOW TO USE YOUR QUIZ RESULTS

Your quiz results can help you begin to see which challenges you struggle with most and point to the skills you most need to build to outsmart your smartphone. To better understand your results, look over your scores. A low score suggests you have built that particular skill fairly well; a high score suggests you still struggle with that particular skill.

If a few scores stand out as being especially high *for you*, then pay special attention to the steps (chapters) that focus on those skills, do the activities several times, and push yourself to practice these skills in your daily life more often. If all of your scores on the quiz are about the same, you'll still benefit from putting extra effort into just a couple skills to start. So choose one or two skills to prioritize, perhaps the ones that seem most important or most enjoyable *to you*. Your goal here is to spend more of your time and effort learning the skills you're likely to benefit from the most. By prioritizing the skills that are likely to make the biggest impact *for you*, you can outsmart your smartphone more quickly and easily. But don't worry if you're not exactly sure what to focus on—just keep reading, and I'll walk you through the process step-by-step.

FINAL THOUGHTS

The truth is that building happiness now, in the presence of our smartphones, can be a tricky task. But soon you'll see why it is not an impossible task. There are lots of skills you can build, strategies you can implement, and things you can do to outsmart your smartphone and live a happy, balanced, more connected life. Are you ready for this to become your reality? Then let's talk about the true causes of unhappiness in the technology age so you'll know why we need to take the seven steps outlined in this book.

Smartphone Syndrome

We grew up watching Disney movies, adventure stories, and comedies that almost always resulted in a "happily ever after." We saw images of buff men and skinny women, never with a hair out of place. And we were told about the American dream—the idea that with hard work, you can achieve anything. So we expected that we too could achieve these things—the happy marriage, the attractive body, the good job— and that these things would bring us happiness. I did, anyway. That is until "happily ever after" blew up in my face.

After spending a decade busting my butt, finally I was done with my PhD, and it was time to get a job. Over the course of several months, I submitted more than one hundred applications, interviewed at sixteen different companies, and had thirty-six interviews in all… but I got zero job offers. Defeated and demoralized, I deferred my grad- uation so I could keep my health insurance and pay my rent.

Meanwhile, at home, my marriage was falling apart. We barely spoke, but the resentment in our eyes said it all. I dreaded coming home, every day wondering if the marriage would make it another day. So, at what was supposed to be this "happily ever after" moment in my life, I was completely miserable.

What's worse, I blamed myself. As a student studying happiness, I was taught to believe that my happiness was entirely in my control. I had in fact learned tons of scientifically supported ways to increase my own happiness. So I strongly believed that I could pull out these strate- gies whenever I needed them, and voila, happiness would just magi- cally appear. These strategies actually *do* work sometimes, and they had worked for me plenty of times in the past…but they didn't work this time. This time, none of these evidence-based happiness-boosting strategies were making me happy.

Eventually, I started to question the modern self-help paradigm: *Do we really have the power to "help ourselves"?* I wondered, if millions of dollars' worth of self-help books, courses, and workshops are sold each year, why then are so many of us still so unhappy? It just didn't add up. There had to be something that I was missing—*something* must be stopping us from finding happiness with existing strategies.

WHAT HAPPENED TO HAPPINESS?

If you look at just about any statistic, you'll see that we're not as happy as we used to be. Depression and anxiety symptoms are up (Mojtabai, Olfson, and Han 2016; Twenge 2000). Suicide and self-harm rates are up. Overdose- and alcohol-related deaths are up (Case and Deaton 2015). And even though many of us are not struggling with these major mental health issues, most of us *are* struggling in our own seemingly small, yet significant ways. Maybe our chronic self-doubt keeps us from enjoying our life. Maybe we need a couple glasses of wine each night just to de-stress. Or maybe our persistent feeling of loneliness leads us to compulsively check our social media accounts. Most of us now have this nagging sense that *something* isn't right…but we can't quite put our finger on what the actual problem is.

It turns out it's really hard to know what, exactly, is making us unhappy because the causes of unhappiness are complex, multifaceted, and often invisible. If some guy punches you in the face, you totally understand why your face hurts. But what about when your heart hurts? Where does *that* pain come from? Is it because you're not positive, mindful, or resilient enough? Is it because your job or relationship really suck? Or is it because of something bigger—the general erosion of kindness, connection, and meaning in our technology-obsessed world?

Well, what I discovered when I went through the most challenging time in my life is that happiness—and therefore unhappiness—comes from all three of these things simultaneously. Unhappiness can originate from inside us—for example, from a poor ability to be mindful or think positive. It can come from the situations we're in—like being in a stressful job or marriage. Or, unhappiness can come from what's happening in the world all around us—for example, it can come from a technology-obsessed world that is constantly changing the ways we pursue important goals like happiness, balance, and connection. So if just one of these causes of unhappiness exists in your life, you're not going to be as happy as you could be.

Unfortunately, most self-help tools—books, workshops, coaching, and so forth—focus exclusively on the unhappiness that comes from inside us. We'll rarely hear that the difficult situations we're dealing with also affect our happiness—our job that expects us to be reachable on our smartphone 24-7, our culture that now finds it acceptable for smartphones to interrupt every conversation, and our ever-accessible media that bombards us with messages that we never have enough and are never good enough. No wonder we're unhappy, right?!

So how do we overcome this giant challenge? Well, we first need to step back and ask ourselves a very important question: What *really* leads to unhappiness in the technology age? Only when we understand the *real* underlying causes of our unhappiness can we start to address these causes and find the true happiness that we seek. So let's start to explore these causes.

In this chapter, we'll discuss:

- what causes unhappiness in the technology age

- how technology gives us unrealistic expectations

- why tech-based solutions for unhappiness aren't working.

WHAT CAUSES UNHAPPINESS IN THE TECHNOLOGY AGE?

Of course, unhappiness has been around a long time. But now, in the technology age, it's spreading like wildfire. When a large number of people all struggle with the same thing—in this case, unhappiness—it suggests that at least some of the causes are *not* inside of us as individuals (in other words, not our thoughts, feelings, or actions). Rather, the causes are things outside us—things that are affecting all of us at once. And that's exactly what's been happening over the last several decades.

We wouldn't all get more stressed, depressed, and unhappy at the same time unless there was some external cause. So to figure out what's causing *our* unhappiness, we first need to figure what is causing unhappiness more generally. We need to look outside of ourselves into our world and ask: *What's different?*

Over the last half century, access to modern technology—the TV, Internet, and smartphones—has exploded. This new era, characterized by development and use of this modern technology, is sometimes deemed "the technology age." In the technology age, the way we make our living, the ways we connect with others, and even how we spend our time is heavily influenced by technology. Maybe we spend all day in front of a computer screen or make our income working "gigs" for one of the giant technology companies—ride-giving, task-doing, room-renting, and the like. Maybe we socialize mostly on our smartphone—emailing, messaging, or chatting on social media. Or maybe we relax by consuming media, perhaps even more than one type of media at a time—for example, watching TV while using our smartphone or texting a friend while we surf the Internet.

Technology has fundamentally changed our lives (Roberts and Foehr 2008). The unintended consequence is that technology has also fundamentally changed our happiness.

How Technology Is Killing the American Dream

Only ten years ago, I stood behind an old brown cash register, sliding purchases across a crisscross red scanner at a local retail store. My hands were that familiar brown color after having touched thousands of dusty products and piling them in plastic bags for customers. My feet ached from standing in a three-square-foot space for eight hours a day—eight hours that earned me $7.25 an hour (minimum wage at the time) or approximately $46 after taxes.

On the surface, things didn't look so bad. My day-to-day job stress was pretty low. I liked my coworkers and often enjoyed my work tasks. But I felt trapped. And after years of unsuccessful attempts to get a better paying job, I started to feel hopeless. I couldn't afford to go back to school. I didn't have health care. I could barely afford my mortgage. Ultimately, I lost my job and then my home.

My experience is not at all unusual. In fact, it is the norm. What is unusual is that I got a lucky break. I met the right people, ended up getting into a fully-funded master's program, later got into a PhD program at Berkeley, and now I'm writing this book. I am living the American dream—the dream that if we work hard, we can achieve anything. But it's actually a really weird experience because I feel like I'm the only one. Neither the people I grew up with nor the people I interact with now ever experienced this upward trajectory. And it's at least in part because technology is killing the American dream.

Technology automated more and more jobs and enabled other jobs to be outsourced, while the cost of living—housing, education, and health care—has skyrocketed. The majority of people now worry, at least a little bit, about how they'll pay for food, or health care, or housing. Others have a vague anxiety that something bad could happen—a health crisis, a job loss, or a family member in need of financial support. Then what? Will we keep our health care? Will we be able to pay our bills? Will we have a place to live? Even those of us who are doing okay right now know that we're just surviving, not thriving.

The low-level chronic stress that this experience creates erodes happiness slowly and insidiously. And this stress is caused, at least in part, by technology. It's an example of why you can build a bunch of happiness skills—mindfulness, gratitude, and so forth—and still end up unhappy. And it's part of the reason why fixing our unhappiness, now in the technology age, requires we focus not only on *self*-improvement but also on *social*-improvement. The causes of unhappiness are not just inside us; they are in the world around us.

How Technology Destroyed Our Sense of Security

In recent years, technology has enabled us to work remotely for businesses all over the globe. In some ways, this is great. We have more access to jobs, and jobs have more access to us. But along with this technology-driven change in how we work has come a lack of stable employment (Mulcahy 2016). Near half of us have spent some time as a freelancer, consultant, or contractor—independent workers in the so-called "gig economy." Others work perpetual part-time jobs. And the rest of us know that our employers could drop us at a moment's notice. As a result, 78 percent of us are living paycheck to paycheck (Dickler 2017).

These changes have been sold to us as a boon to our freedom, flexibility, and independence. But are they really? Sure, you can make your own schedule—perhaps driving people around at night or picking up side work on the weekend. But how relaxed can you be if you can't afford to pay your bills? How strong can your relationships be if you don't have time to see the people you love? How mindful can you be if becoming more self-aware means that you're now aware that any day could be the day you don't make enough money to support yourself or your family? Our lives are now chronically uncertain, and there is just no way that practicing a little bit of self-help can combat that kind of stress.

In fact, chronic uncertainty can break us—not today or tomorrow, but one day at a time. Life no longer feels predictable—and it isn't. We can end up feeling powerless (Ferrie et al. 1998), and as a result, we become more vigilant—we're more cautious of things that could hurt us mentally or physically, for example, the people who are different than us, a rapidly changing world, or even divergent opinions that might threaten our identity.

Our bodies generate extra stress hormones to help us prepare for possible threats, and soon we become chronically stressed. This stress is good in small doses because it protects us. But chronic stress—whether it is because of work, money, or something else entirely—limits the amount of happiness we can create for ourselves because it pervades our entire lives and everything we do. Maybe we get annoyed with our family, cry for no reason, or become exhausted and unable to recuperate. In the technology age, this underlying chronic stress is affecting us all.

So what do we do? Focusing our attention inward, with techniques like mindfulness or deep breathing, can be helpful. But interestingly, focusing our attention outward to connect and be kind to others actually seems to be even more helpful. The great secret of happiness is that the actions we take to make the world a better place are the exact same actions that tend to be most effective at increasing our *personal* happiness.

How Technology Eroded Our Social Support Systems

Another major underlying cause of unhappiness in the technology age is the loss of our social support systems. With the advent of the TV, then video games, the personalized computer, and now the smartphone, we are spending more and more time with technologies and less and less time with other human beings. Simultaneously, more of us are living alone or with fewer people than we used to (Holt-Lunstad, Robles, and Sbarra 2017). A growing number of us work at home—interacting with coworkers, customers, or clients only through technologies like cell phones, video chat, or the Internet. And we don't do as many social activities as we used to do—things like volunteering, going to church, or even chatting with neighbors (Holt-Lunstad, Robles, and Sbarra 2017, Guest and Wierzbicki 1999). Altogether, the size of our social communities has declined by a third over the last thirty years (Holt-Lunstad, Robles, and Sbarra 2017).

As a result of the way we now live in the technology age, more and more people feel lonely and isolated. Many of us have few people to reach out to if we need a hug, an ear to listen, or even just a buddy to meet up with. So we struggle alone, spend even more time with our technology toys to cope with our loneliness, and get sucked into a technology-induced downward spiral that we have no idea how to pull ourselves out of.

Luckily, we *can* pull ourselves out of our technology-induced lone-liness spiral precisely by doing the opposite actions that got us here. For example, volunteer, play sports with others, or do something else social. The result of these actions is that we can start to regain the social resources that we've lost in the technology age and rediscover our happiness.

HOW TECHNOLOGY GAVE US UNREALISTIC EXPECTATIONS

Technology has not only impacted our society. Technology has also made it infinitely easier to deliver media to us all day and all night—media that tends to set us up for all sorts of unhappiness traps. These traps fundamentally change our expectations, leading us to believe that nothing in our lives is ever good enough. Now, because of the ubiquity of technology, we fall into these traps so slowly and at such a young age that they are completely invisible to us. Even when we're caught in one of these unhappiness traps, it's hard to tell because we've been there so long that we've forgotten (or never knew) what it feels like to be free from it.

The Envy Trap

We are spending more and more of our time on social media. We express ourselves, engage with others, and communicate with other people online. But who *are* we when we're online? Our profiles are more like a fantasy—an image of who we want to be, not an image of who we actually are. We broadcast only our most exciting, flattering, best news (Panger 2017), so the posts, stories, and pictures we see on social media are just collections of only the awesomest moments in our lives—not a collection of our real, deep, and authentic moments.

I'm not above it. I post when I get the job—not when I don't get a job I really wanted. I post when I look at a beautiful landscape—not when I look at my boring computer screen (which is what I *really* spend most my time looking at). I only post pictures of my partner and me when we're happy. It's not like I pause in the middle of an argument to say, "Wait, let me snap a selfie while we yell at each other." We present the best versions of ourselves so "the good side" is the only side of us that people ever see (Panger 2014), and it's the only side of them that we see. Then, because it's human nature, we compare ourselves to the best versions of everyone else (Morse and Gergen 1970).

What do you think happens when we compare ourselves, flaws and all, to "the good side" of everyone else? Occasionally, we might be inspired to become better versions of ourselves. Maybe we see that a colleague lost fifteen pounds, and suddenly we realize that we too can achieve our weight loss goal. Or maybe we see someone volunteering their time to a good cause, and we decide that we too want to give back in ways that matter to us. But more often, when we compare ourselves to only the best parts of others, we come up short (Hagerty 2000). And we end up feeling crappy about ourselves.

You know the feeling; it's like when your friend posts pictures of a beautiful beach vacation with the love of their life, but you're still dating duds. Or when your former classmate suddenly gets their dream job, but you're still struggling to make ends meet. Or when your friend posts a perfectly Photoshopped selfie while you try to hide that giant pimple that popped up on your nose. Seeing other people's most positive moments on social media often ends up making us feel inferior (I suck!) or envious (they suck!) or both (Krasnova et al. 2013). So the more we use social media, the more we think our lives suck (Steers,

Wickham, and Acitelli 2014), and the worse we feel. We're unhappy, and we can't figure out why.

The Romance Trap

Another trap that we may fall into is set by romantic comedy, sitcoms, and Disney movies, which frequently depict exaggerated plot lines and unrealistic outcomes. In these movies and shows, the relationships are full of romance, intimacy, and passion—often merging the best aspects of both new relationships and longer-term relationships. We see lots of compliments, gift-giving, and affection. But this isn't an accurate portrayal of what real, healthy relationships are actually like (Johnson and Holmes 2009).

Why does it matter? It probably didn't matter so much a hundred years ago. But now, in the technology age, we're exposed to *a lot* more media, hours of it every day, likely from the time we were in diapers. As youngsters, we didn't have any other experiences to teach us about relationships, so we believed, at least a little bit, that this is what relationships were supposed to be like (Johnson and Holmes 2009; Cohen and Weimann 2000). Maybe we started to believe a good partner was someone who never got mad, who always listened, or who always knew exactly what we wanted. As a result, we formed expectations that couldn't possibly be met, and our happiness suffered because of our unrealistic expectations.

The Sexuality Trap

Another trap we fall into is set by pornography, a genre of media that is now accessible 24-7, both to children and adults. Not very long ago, pornography was hard to find, even among highly motivated teenage boys. But now, with increased access to the Internet, the *majority* of young people learn about sex from pornography. Like romantic comedy, pornography creates unrealistic expectations about what sexual relationships are really like.

So what expectations do we have now that our world has been consumed by pornography? Well, we see perfectly manicured bodies. We see perfect sexual performance (Bridges et al. 2010). And we see degrading and violent behaviors toward women. The problem here is that these interactions don't tend to be representative of loving, healthy sexual relationships. (Sun et al. 2016). But just like romantic comedies, viewing this media gives us unrealistic expectations about what healthy sexual relationships are supposed to be like. So the more we watch, the more we apply what we learn in real world interactions, the less satisfied we are with ourselves, and the less satisfied we are with our relationships (Sun et al. 2016; Park et al. 2016). We end up thinking that our sexual relationships (and our partner) should be different than they are—our expectations have trapped us again. And we may have a difficult time being happy because what we want, and think we deserve, doesn't actually exist.

Getting Out of Happiness Traps Set by Media

Given that technology is decreasing our happiness overall while simultaneously creating sky-high expectations, the distance between how happy we are and how happy we want to be continues to grow. We now have a distorted image of the happiness we desire—a sort of "super happiness" that includes the perfect life, the perfect partner, and perfect sex, which makes us exceedingly happy…all the time. But this is not at all what *true* happiness is. If we keep shooting for something that doesn't exist, we're never going to get it. That's why increasing happiness in the technology age requires we first define happiness, and then pursue it, in a more realistic way.

WHY TECH-BASED SOLUTIONS FOR UNHAPPINESS AREN'T WORKING

Following only slightly behind the massive growth of smartphones and social media, another technology industry is now growing rapidly. This industry consists of tech-based solutions for unhappiness: the apps, courses, platforms, devices, and other technology-based tools designed to help you improve happiness and other mental health-related issues. I have spent the last few years working in this industry with the hope that these tech-based solutions would solve all of our unhappiness problems. Indeed, they are affordable and scalable and have high-potential for positive impact. But recently I've started to wonder, *Is more technology really the solution to the problems caused by technology?* Unfortunately, the longer I work in this industry, the more I see the many problems that still need to be overcome before these tech-based solutions help us in the ways we really need them to.

Tech-Based Solutions for Unhappiness Can Harm Us

Not all tech-based solutions for unhappiness are harmful—not at all! But I worry that any benefit we gain from the helpful tech-based solutions is canceled out by the harmful ones.

Why are some of these tech-based solutions harmful? One reason is that most people don't think they can fix a car, or mend a broken arm, or a cure a physical ailment, but a surprising number of people think that they can fix unhappiness, even if they've never formally studied happiness in their lives. So, the people who have true expertise in this area are rarely the ones building tech-based solutions for unhappiness. This problem is akin to having doctors who have never actually worked with a patient or mechanics who have never actually fixed a car.

The fact that nonexperts make the majority of tech-based solutions for unhappiness is a major problem because people often "don't know what they don't know" (Dunning 2011). And humans are *especially* bad at guessing what will lead to happiness (Ford and Mauss 2014). As a result, the evidence suggests that these tech-based solutions for unhappiness might actually be hurting your happiness instead of helping it. For example, the majority of tech-based solutions teach us how to build happiness using self-focused activities (versus other-focused activities). But the research shows that this approach is less effective for increasing happiness, and potentially even damaging in some cases (Ingram 1990). So if you use tech-based solutions for unhappiness that don't have strong science behind them, you may be doing yourself more harm than good.

Another issue with many tech-based solutions for unhappiness is that they capitalize on trends more than science. For example, currently the most popular tech-based solutions focus on mindfulness. But it turns out that when compared to other happiness-boosting strategies, mindfulness doesn't work as well (or quickly) as other techniques (Moltrecht et al. 2014; Kim 2014; Shallcross et al. 2015). Although mindfulness absolutely does have useful applications, if you focus *primarily* on mindfulness, it could have an opportunity cost—if you're using a strategy that helps a little instead of a strategy that helps a lot, you won't increase your happiness as much as you could have.

Maybe this problem seems small—if you're a little less happy than you could have been, it's not the end of the world. But these are the types of problems that keep me up at night. Why? Because *tons* of people use these tech-based solutions to fix their unhappiness, all of them are a little less happy than they could have been, and as a result, our society as a whole is quite a bit less happy than it could have been. And remember, our happiness is driven by what's happening inside us *and* outside of us—in our families, workplaces, communities, and society. So these seemingly small loses of happiness across many individuals likely have ripple effects that prevent us *all* from being as happy as we could have been.

Tech-Based Solutions for Unhappiness Often Make Happiness Seem Totally Impossible

Another problem with tech-based solutions for unhappiness is that they unintentionally make it seem like happiness is totally impossible. For example, you've probably heard some combination of: eat healthy, exercise, meditate, spend time with friends, be more resilient, get outside, be productive, and oh yeah, do all this while doing everything else you have to do just to survive.

I have to do all that to be happy!? Well then, I'm screwed, we might think. It's not that any of this advice is wrong exactly. It's just not realistic. Tech-based solutions for unhappiness can be huge, broad, and so thorough that they often end up using a throw-everything-at-it-including-the-kitchen-sink approach. As a result, you might end up thinking that you must do *all of this* to be happy, which isn't really true anyway.

When using these tech-based solutions for unhappiness (and other solutions as well) you are also likely to hear: "You have the power to increase your own happiness"—a slogan that suggests that your happiness is *entirely* up to you. This message is bound to set you up for disappointment because, as we discussed earlier, some of the causes of unhappiness are outside of you.

If you're a real type A person, like I am, you'll internalize the kitchen-sink approach and the message that your happiness is entirely up to you, and you'll try to do everything you're told to do to be happier. It doesn't lead to the "super happiness" that society has told you is real (but isn't), you blame yourself for failing because supposedly "You have the power to increase your own happiness," and you burn yourself out in the process by trying to do "all the things." This is exactly what happened to me before I gave up on the old self-help paradigm and started looking for a better way to find happiness, balance, and true connection in the technology age.

Luckily, there *is* a better way. Instead of adopting the message that you have complete control over your happiness, think of unhappiness like you're trying to avoid getting the flu during a really bad flu season. Sometimes technology will hurt your happiness in ways you cannot control (just like you might get the flu when it's going around). But there *are* things you *can* do to reduce the likelihood of unhappiness (just like there are things you can do to prevent yourself getting the flu). You may get a bit unhappy from time to time, but if you build the *right* "happiness skills," you'll be less likely to get the unhappiness bug, and it'll be easier to stay happy, even when everyone else isn't. The seven-step program that shows you exactly how to do this is now just right around the corner!

FINAL THOUGHTS

As you just discovered, the causes of, and solutions to, unhappiness are more complicated now in the age of technology. New underlying causes of unhappiness are emerging—they are the side effects of a digital economy, omnipresent access to media, and a lack of technologies that effectively increase happiness. But now that you know why happiness has become so hard to build in the technology age, I think you'll see why my seven-step program may actually work for you. It'll help you overcome the many obstacles that prevent happiness in the technology age. And you won't even have to give up your smartphone.

Build Foundational Skills

It was my last year in college, and I needed to take physics to graduate. I hadn't taken physics in high school, so I was nervous about taking college-level physics. Reluctantly, I signed up. After only one week, I was completely lost. I read the textbook, went to office hours, and attended a study group, but I just kept falling further behind. I even started to get stressed-out when I went to that class. *Could I ever learn physics?* I wondered. In the end, I just barely passed the class. And I never went near physics again.

It's not uncommon for us to give up on something if we aren't successful. When we try to learn something new without knowing the foundational skills, we struggle, get frustrated, and eventually quit. We quit because we *have* learned something—we've learned that we can't possibly learn this darn thing. So we figure, why try? We must just be stupid or broken or something.

Educators know this. This is why the difficulty of classes in school increases a little bit at a time. Most courses require prerequisites. Even in karate, the color of your belt prevents you from getting your butt kicked by someone more advanced than you. We start at the beginning so we can advance more effectively. Yet for some reason, this common sense is rarely applied to learning happiness, even though happiness is a skill too and needs to be built slowly, just like every other skill.

In this chapter, you'll begin at the beginning, by learning the foundational happiness skills. The foundational skills are not necessarily the easiest skills to learn. Rather, they are the prerequisites—the skills that can make it easier to progress successfully through the rest of this book. Sometimes the basics are boring, but they're important because they can help you reach your happiness goals faster and more efficiently. And if these skills seem easy, that's okay too. It just means you'll more easily learn the harder skills that come later on.

In this chapter, you'll:

- set up systems for success

- build a growth mindset

- find balance.

SET UP SYSTEMS FOR SUCCESS

When you first start working toward a new goal—like happiness—you may get a burst of motivation. Suddenly, you have the energy to run on the treadmill four hours per day, eat only healthy food, or read ten books on how to be happier. Eventually, though, your motivation *will* run out. This is to be expected because it turns out that motivation is a limited resource (Baumeister, Vohs, and Tice 2007). But long-term happiness, just like long-term physical health, comes about as a result of making long-term lifestyle changes. You have to keep practicing the skills you've built or else you'll slide back to wherever you started. So how do you do this without relying on motivation?

To keep yourself moving forward, even after motivation has run out, it's essential that you set up systems to keep yourself on track (Fogg 2009). By doing so, you'll have an easier time outsmarting your smartphone, not just today, but also in a month, in a year, and in ten years. Without setting up these systems, you can still finish this book feeling happier. But soon you'll forget to practice the skills you built, over time they will fade, and eventually, you'll end up back where you started. This is why setting up simple systems early on in your pursuit of happiness is really important. And lucky for us, technology makes it super easy to set up these systems. Here's what to do.

Set Up Your "Why"

Clarifying *why* you want to improve your life can help you stay focused and motivated, even on those days when you want to abandon the whole thing. And believe me, you will have those days. I'm having one right now. I made plans to go spend time with a friend this evening, but now that I'm thinking of all the stuff I have to do, part of me really wants to cancel. The only thing stopping me from canceling is my *why*. I made a plan to meet up with my friend because it's important to me to maintain my social connections and lead the kind of life that generates happiness. It can be easy to forget these reasons when the busyness of life gets in the way, but setting up your *why* can really help.

If you remember your *why*, you'll be more likely to make happiness-building decisions in those difficult moments when you want to just revert to your old behaviors (Sheldon and Houser-Marko 2001). So the goal here is to clarify your why and keep it easily accessible as a reminder. Since most of us have our smartphones (or tablets or laptops) near us almost all the time, we now have an opportunity to keep our *why* with us at all times.

So, take a few minutes now to think about your *why*. Why are you working on outsmarting your smartphone? Why is this important to you? How would it affect your life if you kept at it? Write your answers down in your notebook. (Reminder: You'll need a journaling app on your phone or a paperbound notebook for several writing activities in this book.) Whenever you're wavering on doing what you promised yourself you would do, like I am today, reread your *why*.

Set Up Your "When"

If you wanted to speak a new language, play a new instrument, or learn any other new skills, you would have to set aside time to practice these skills. The same thing is true for building the skills that'll help you outsmart your smartphone. The clearer you are about exactly *when* you will build your skills, the more likely it is you will put in the time it takes to actually build these skills.

So take a few minutes now to write a list in your notebook, noting all the chunks of free time you have. Maybe you have five minutes while waiting in line at Starbucks. Maybe you have twenty minutes while riding the bus to work. Maybe you have an hour on Saturday mornings. Choose at least one of these time slots to schedule your "happiness time"—a time that you will devote to your happiness each week. Use whatever tool you rely on to keep track of your other activities, meetings, or events, for example, an online calendar or alarm on your phone.

Don't worry if you only have small chunks of time. What is important is that you have a *regular time scheduled*, a time that you honor just like you would honor any of your other engagements. If that means it will only be ten minutes per week, that's totally fine as long as you stick to it! For now, you can read this book during that time. And once you learn the activities in this book, you can then schedule these activities during your happiness time.

Make a Commitment

We are such silly humans. Sometimes the littlest things make us more likely to succeed in reaching our goals. We don't like to let ourselves down or feel like liars, so one little way we help ourselves stick to our goals is by making a written commitment to stick to them.

Take a few minutes now to make a commitment to outsmart your smartphone. Use your *why* and *when* from the previous sections to clarify exactly what you're committing to. Write and complete the following statement in your notebook.

I, _____ (name), am dedicated to outsmarting my smartphone because _____ (why), and I will reach this goal by practicing the skills that generate happiness _____ (when).

Signature _____ Date _____

Add a reminder in your calendar or phone to reread your commitment once per month so it stays fresh in your mind.

Once you've done this, you've set up your simple systems. The rest of this book will help you figure out what skill-building activities, exactly, to schedule during your happiness time. The first and most foundational of these skills are described in the next sections.

BUILD A GROWTH MINDSET

I was painfully shy growing up—the kind of child who hid behind her mom's legs when strangers were around. I hated even raising my hand in class let alone presenting in front of the whole room. So in college, when I gave my first presentation, my hands were visibly shaking, my heart on fire, and my voice squeaky. Yeah, I totally sucked. But I believed I could get better, so I kept at it. Each time I presented, I *did* get better, even if just a tiny bit. Despite still being that quiet introvert who gets nervous in front of an audience, after a few years, I ended up actually being decent at public speaking. How did this happen? I *believed* I could improve, so I kept *trying* to improve.

Now, what do you think would have happened if I didn't believe I could improve? This is what happened to my friend Henry (not his real name). He too struggled with public speaking. The only difference between him and me was that he was convinced that he would *always* struggle with public speaking. He avoided opportunities that would help him improve, and as a result, he didn't improve. He didn't *believe* he could get better, and this sabotaged his success.

The belief that you can grow and improve, often referred to as growth mindset, has a surprisingly big impact on your ability to reach your goals. In fact, the more you believe that you can improve a skill, the more likely it is that you actually will improve that skill (Dweck 2009). And you know what's really neat? This belief also applies to your happiness (Duckworth et al. 2007; Dweck 2009; Tamir et al. 2007). Believing that you *can* build your happiness makes it more likely that you will. How come? Well, it's not magic. It's because if you don't believe happiness is possible for you, then you won't put in the necessary hard work that is required to build it. But, if you do believe happiness is possible for you, then it suddenly seems totally worth the effort, and you start working your butt off to get it (Dweck 2009).

In the past, it would have been nearly impossible to learn skills, like growth mindset, that people in our immediate social network didn't know. But now, there is a ton of information online—and lots of information on how to build happiness. So we *can* do it, as long as we both believe we *can* do it and put in the effort.

Luckily for me, most of the people who seek out my help already believe happiness is possible—if they didn't, why would they be trying? You're reading this book, so you too likely believe, at least a little bit, that you can outsmart your smartphone and be happier. But for a variety of reasons, many of us still struggle with maintaining this belief over the long haul. So if you if you start to waver, come back and do the following activity.

Shift Your Mindset

If you're like many people, you occasionally have doubts about your ability to build your happiness. Maybe you've failed before, and now you are rightfully skeptical about all this hype around "having the power to change your life!" But remember, happiness is just a set of skills. Once we shift our mindset to thinking of happiness as a skill set, it doesn't seem quite as elusive. You've learned a zillion other skills before—riding a bike, cooking a meal, playing a sport, and so on—and you can learn happiness skills too.

To shift to this mindset, first, take a few moments to think about one time you learned a new skill. Maybe you learned how to play chess. Maybe you learned how to fix a car. Or maybe you learned how to code. If you want to push yourself, you can even try to recall when you learned happiness skills. Maybe you learned how to communicate better when you feel angry. Maybe you learned to stop eating pints of ice cream when you feel sad. Maybe you learned to text a friend when you feel lonely. Now, choose one skill you built and write it down in your notebook.

Next, ask yourself the following questions. How did you learn this skill? What challenges did you have to overcome? Did you progress in a linear fashion, or did you go through rapid improvement followed by periods of slow improvement or even backsliding? Reflect on your answers here, paying especial attention to the core truth that you *can* build new skills, even if it's hard sometimes.

Keep in mind that a single use of this activity (or any other activity in this book) will not result in permanent changes in your brain. Just like when you built other skills, you had to do the activities many times to create permanent changes. So if at any point in the program you feel like you've stopped believing that you can increase your happiness, come back and do this activity again. With this foundational skill, you'll have an easier time moving forward with all the other skills in this book.

FIND BALANCE

Finding balance was one of the hardest skills for me to learn. While pursuing my PhD, I lost all sight of a balanced life. Amidst schoolwork, I also started a business. When my business started failing, I thought I could fix it by working harder. But before long, I started getting migraines, insomnia, and back pain. I stopped valuing and prioritizing the people in my life, even neglecting to spend time with my partner and my friends. I felt aimless, and I started wondering why I didn't feel like my life had any meaning. Little by little, the quality of my work started to decline. I scheduled meetings at the wrong times, wrote articles that were missing lots of words, and I couldn't answer the simplest of questions. In short: I was burnt out (Schutte et al. 2000).

If that wasn't bad enough, an odd thing happened when my life was out of balance. All of my other happiness skills completely stopped working. I just didn't have the energy to think and behave in ways that were good for me. My brain was so tired it reverted to old patterns and couldn't build new ones. If you've struggled in the past to build the skills that lead to happiness—skills like positivity, mindfulness, and resilience—you likely need to focus on rebuilding your energy by creating a more balanced life.

So how do you create balance and sustain your energy? Well, first you need to split your time between different parts of your life. Just like a plant that needs adequate doses of different nutrients to thrive, you too need a variety of different experiences—things like personal time, social time, and yes, even work time to thrive. If one part is missing, the other parts suffer too. When you find a good balance between these different parts of your life, a strange thing happens: you end up enjoying *all* of your experiences more. That's the brilliance of balance.

Unfortunately, in the technology age, balance has become exponentially harder to find. Technology has made it easy for all the aspects of our lives to contaminate the others. We check email first thing in the morning and last thing at night. Our coworkers and to-do lists follow us wherever we go, often pinging us repeatedly, intruding on time that we've set aside for something else. We're now convinced that that we need to be connected to technology at all times—we can no longer imagine leaving the house without our phone, skipping a day of email, or taking a week off from social media.

Instead of confronting the reality that personal time cannot also be work time, some of us have embraced a semi-fictional belief that we can get work done while still participating fully in the other important aspects of our lives. We think we can answer just a few work emails while we enjoy our beach vacation. We think we can take that important phone call in the evening, as long as it's not at the dinner table. We think we can even "talk shop" while we enjoy happy hour with colleagues. It seems like we can do all the things we want and need to do simultaneously without having to sacrifice anything. But are we just kidding ourselves?

The truth is that choosing to answer a work-related call or email during your personal time interrupts the flow of conversation, pulls you out of the present moment, and shifts your mind away from what balances and nourishes you. It may seem innocuous—it's just a couple minutes after all—but there are real impacts on your happiness. This is why balance, in the technology age, means more than setting aside time for the many parts of our lives; it also means guarding that time vigorously.

So how do you make sure your life is, and stays, in balance?

Devote More Time to Doing Things That Energize You

When you notice something is draining your energy, it might be a sign that something is out of balance. We feel drained because the mental resources we have for that particular activity are depleted and other more stimulating parts of our life aren't recharging us. So first, we need to figure out what *does* energize us and devote a bit more time to those things.

That's sometimes easier said than done though because each of us is energized by different things. Some people are energized by being around other people; others are energized by being alone. Some like art, and some like sports. Some like activities that are part of a routine, and others like to do things that are out of the ordinary. What about you?

Take a few moments now to think about all the activities that energize you. Write this list down in your notebook. As you're writing, keep these guidelines in mind:

- *Be specific.* For example, write, "Go to Bobby's Café with Alex," instead of just writing, "See Alex."

- *Be thorough.* For example, write down activities you could do in different life domains including work and school, family and friends, clubs and hobbies, and so forth.

- *Be strategic.* For example, if you are energized by both relaxation and spending time with friends, you could plan a spa day with Sarah, helping you recharge in two different ways.

Got your list? Right now, before you forget, take a moment to schedule at least one of these activities. If you need to coordinate with other people, call, text, or email them now. Do you feel like you're just too busy and you couldn't possibly fit this into your packed schedule? Feel free to schedule these activities a few weeks or even months out if you need to. And don't forget, you can schedule them during your happiness time—the time you already set aside for your happiness.

Keep in mind that you can increase the energy boost you get from these activities by doing them more frequently. So whenever possible, schedule these activities to repeat each week or month. For example, you could plan to play racquetball with Jared at 3:00 p.m. every Saturday or get brunch with Pat the first Sunday of every month. This is a great way to make good use of technology tools like online calendars or productivity apps—you can set your planned activities to repeat as often as you like and even add a reminder so you don't forget. By marking down the times you plan to spend doing the things you love with the people you love, the more likely it will be that you'll actually do them.

Set Stronger Boundaries

These days, everyone says they are "too busy" or "too exhausted." That may be true, but the problem with hearing people say this all the time is that it leads us to feel like we too should be working all the time—and at breakneck speed. This was very much a part of what led to my burnout. No one ever explicitly told me I had to be available 24-7, but if I failed to answer an email for even a few hours, I'd get a follow up email asking me why I hadn't yet responded to the previous one. I'd turn in reports and be asked redo them again and again, even if that meant working nights and weekends. Once, I even skipped a family vacation because I felt pressured to work instead.

At the time, I didn't think it was possible to set any boundaries. *It was just part of the job*, I told myself. But when I eventually stepped back and really thought about each of the tasks I was doing late at night or on weekends—tasks that were tearing me away from my friends, family, and hobbies—I realized that very few tasks really mattered that much. They weren't so urgent or important that they deserved *all* of my time or to be handled *right away*.

What about you? Do you often feel like work is encroaching on your personal time? If so, take a moment now to think about the types of tasks you have done on evenings, weekends, vacations, or during other times that you hoped to recharge. Write these tasks in your notebook. Note which of these tasks are really urgent and which could be put off for later. Ask yourself, "What would I need to say no to maintain good boundaries between work and personal time?" Use this list next time your recharge time is intruded upon to decide what you will and won't do.

Next, ask yourself what kind of life you want to lead. What are you willing and not willing to live with? What experiences will you look back upon and wish that you had engaged in fully? Have you ever regretted being drawn away from time with your family or friends? I tell you, I regret not going on that family vacation to work instead. How will you avoid letting this happen to *you*? Will you turn off your phone during specific hours of the day? Write down your answers to these questions in your notebook.

Keep in mind that finding solutions here is hard, especially in the technology age. There are no quick fixes. And the decisions you make—the decisions that are right for you—might have consequences. Your boss might punish you for enforcing your boundaries, your coworkers may shun you, or your company may decide not to promote you. Believe me, I know what you are up against. After I burnt out, I had to get a different job in order to create the balanced life that I needed to be happy. That was indeed challenging. But that's how we get happier: we do the hard things we need to do to make our lives better. And sometimes, you just might be surprised. Maybe *you* were the only one creating your unbalanced life. Maybe once you make a change, the only thing different will be that you feel a bit more balanced, a bit less stressed, and a bit happier. The only way to know for sure is to give it a try.

Take a Look at How Your Diet Is Affecting Your Emotions

This may come as a surprise, but technology affects the way we eat. Now, with our short attention spans and our desire for stimulation, many of us have become more open and interested in eating a greater variety of foods. Ad campaigns for new foods can reach us more easily, and we can more easily research new foods online. This isn't necessarily a bad thing except that the foods we are most likely to encounter through aggressive ad campaigns, product placement in our favorite shows, and other media don't tend to be foods that are good for us. In fact, these unhealthy foods can not only wreak havoc on your physical health (Walsh 2011), they can also affect physiological processes related to your happiness and well-being.

We often only think of the physical health benefits of eating a healthy diet, but the foods we eat also affect our hormones (Haggans et al. 1999; Anderson et al. 2013), our sleep patterns (Smith 2002), and even the effectiveness of exercise (Malhotra, Noakes, and Phinney 2015)—all things that impact our happiness. So this means that if we don't have a healthy diet, we can do all the work of building new happiness skills and still get stuck feeling unhappy. Our bodies and minds work together and need to support each other.

Of course, health and nutrition are complex subjects that require much more depth than we can go into here. But as a start, take a moment now to reflect on your eating habits in your notebook. Ask yourself: "Do you consume any of the strongest mood-altering substances (caffeine, sugar, alcohol, cigarettes)? Do you consume 'weaker' mood-altering substances (wheat, dairy, carbs, chocolate)? Would you be willing to cut back or even quit some or all of these foods? If not, why not?"

Of course, eliminating these common foods from your diet can be incredibly difficult, but ask yourself, "Is there any way you could quit one or two of these foods for a short time just to see how it makes you feel?" If so, keep in mind that detoxes from these mood-altering substances may lead to withdrawal symptoms at first. Indeed, the benefits to your happiness here do not come quickly and are hard won.

When I first removed mood-altering foods from my diet, I felt exhausted at first. But after a bit, my brain livened up, and I felt more able to be self-reflective. I saw the problems in my life that needed fixing more clearly so I could actually fix them. I was no longer able to fuel unhealthy amounts of work with caffeine, no longer able to cope with unhealthy levels of stress with alcohol, and no longer able to eat sugary treats to fill moments of boredom, anxiety, or sadness. So, instead, I had to actually figure out how live my life in a more satisfying way. This clarity, in addition to the hormonal benefits, is why I believe eating a healthy diet is a key part of creating balance and developing your happiness.

FINAL THOUGHTS

Now that you know the foundations, you're all set-up to be successful throughout the rest of this book. Hopefully, you feel a bit more prepared and have some systems to help keep you on track throughout this whole journey.

Stay Present

In our technology-crazed world, instead of spending even a second alone with our thoughts, we reflexively turn to our cell phones for entertainment, comfort, or distraction. Many of us are on our phones at work, in the bathroom, and even during sex. We let media decide what we believe, we let social media determine how we feel about ourselves, and we let our smartphones determine how we spend our time. We have become so "connected" that we seem to have lost the ability to connect to ourselves and the present in the moment. But this is exactly what we need to do to outsmart our smartphones and start building our happiness.

In this chapter, you'll learn how to limit your technology use, in small ways at first, then in larger ways, giving you some much-needed time to stay present in the moment and reconnect with yourself. These small moments of disconnection from technology give you increasingly more opportunities to be fully present in the moment and finally uncover some of the causes of your distress.

In this chapter, you'll learn how to:

- overcome fear of missing out (FOMO)

- take technology timeouts

- practice being more mindful.

OVERCOME FEAR OF MISSING OUT (FOMO)

Having constant access to our cell phones and the Internet can be really helpful. We can check the weather, read the news, or learn about events wherever we are. But, because we now know of so many things that are going on in other places—online and IRL—we can start to believe we are missing out on fun or important experiences. This feeling is referred to as fear of missing out, or FOMO (Baker, Krieger, and LeRoy 2016), and it can lead us to stay attached to our phones or social media 24-7 just to make sure we don't miss anything.

Although there is nothing inherently wrong with wanting to be where the fun is, having a variety of experiences, and staying up-to-date on the day's happenings, when we are always thinking about what's happening elsewhere, we cannot be fully be present with what-ever is happening right in front of us (Baker, Krieger, and LeRoy 2016). This is why FOMO hurts our happiness and why overcoming it helps us build our happiness.

Reflect on How You Use Technology

Ideally, modern technologies are just used as tools—a phone is for sending and receiving messages, and a computer is for doing necessary tasks. But in recent years, technologies have been increasingly designed to hook you, keeping you from ever putting them away, perhaps even getting you addicted to entertainment, social connection, and even self-aggrandizement. Most of us are blissfully unaware of how reliant we really are on these technologies, not because of their utility but because of the emotional comfort or satisfaction that they provide. The problem is that this comfort is superficial and short-lived. Just as an addict would get great pleasure from consuming their drug of choice, we too get great pleasure from using our technologies. But both are just a distraction from real life, and both have the real potential to take us further away from happiness in the long run.

To increase awareness about your relationship to technology, take a few days to pay attention to your relationship with your phone, computer, TV, video game console, or other technologies that occupy a large portion of your time. Ask yourself the following questions and write down the answers in your notebook.

What emotions do you have before using technology? What do you do when you use technology? Who are you with? What are you doing? Where are you? Are there particular apps you use often? What do you do after using technology? How long do you use it for?

Try to answer these questions a few different times, on a few different days. Once you are done, read over your answers and look for common themes. Ask yourself: "Are you using technology to cope with particular emotions, thoughts, or situations? Do you spend more time using technology than you would like? How does it make you feel in the short term? How about in the longer term?"

If you discover that you, like most of us, are using technology not as a tool to achieve some task, but as a way to cope with or distract yourself from some other experience, be prepared for a challenge up ahead. When we become reliant on (or addicted to) something—anything—to change our emotions, removing that something means that we'll have to face, possibly for the first time in a while, what it feels like to actually experience these emotions. This is very likely to result in cravings—*I'll just check my social media for a minute. What's the harm?* Giving into these cravings only makes them worse because you never get to experience being technology-free for long enough for your brain to learn that it's *okay* and everything is going to be alright.

If you expect you'll have trouble with technology cravings, you can try these deterrents: Set the lock screen on your phone with an image that reminds you not to go further. If you find that you skip through your lock screen, ignoring your reminder, you may need an extra layer of defense. If this sounds like you, then put something on the outside of your phone to slow you down. You could attach a sticker to your phone or place a rubber band around it, a physical barrier that slows you down and reminds you not to proceed. Similar approaches could be used with computers or video game consoles. The goal here is to create a mental or physical barrier that slows you down and makes you pause for a second to think, *Hey, do I really want to do this?* With your improved awareness of the relationship you have to technology, you'll likely have more success overcoming FOMO and have an easier time outsmarting your smartphone.

TAKE TECHNOLOGY TIMEOUTS

If we've got our FOMO under control, we are more easily able to start taking technology timeouts—or short breaks from using our smartphones, computers, or other technology toys. You already know technology is hurting your happiness, but you're not quite sure how. That's why taking these short, but purposeful, #TechnologyTimeouts is essential for outsmarting your smartphone. Without all the distractions, you'll be forced to stay present with yourself and others. And the heightened level of self-awareness is exactly what you need to start turning your life around. Try the following strategies to see which ones have the biggest impact for you.

Take Text Timeouts

Many people, especially young people, sit with their phones between themselves and whatever is in front of them—their computers, their entertainment, or another person who is speaking to them. Does this sound like you? If so, you may be waiting—maybe hoping—that a message will pop up. But if it does, it will immediately take you out of the present moment. You'll miss out on what's happening right in front you. And it turns out that what's happening in our real lives is almost always better for our happiness than what's happening on our phone.

Even if you don't keep your smartphone right in front of you, it's probably nearby—on the table, in a purse or backpack, or in your pocket. And that buzz or bing of a message feels like it needs to be answered immediately. But you know what, it doesn't. Try taking a #TextTimeout, and you'll see for yourself. You quickly discover that it's worth it to wait to answer messages and devote your full attention to what's happening right in front of you. Here's what to do if you want to take a #TextTimeout.

First, let your friends, family, and community know that you're taking a #TextTimeout. You may be so programmed to answer messages immediately that if you don't, the people you care about may take it as a slight. *Why is he or she ignoring me?* they may wonder. So be sure to send out a group message or make a social media post to let folks know you're planning to #OutsmartYourSmartphone and are taking a brief #TextTimeout.

Next, get yourself ready. Most phones give you the option to silence message buzzes and bings in various ways. Now, not everyone can just silence all texts all the time. For your #TextTimeout, it'll be up to you to explore different strategies and decide what works best for your life. But make it your goal to limit texting or messaging in at least one way.

For example, if you often answer messages in the middle of the night, I highly recommend starting your #TextTimeout by silencing all messages during nighttime hours. Your sleep is incredibly important for your happiness, and these tiny disturbances can alter your sleep in important ways. Personally, I have all my notifications turned off between 9:00 p.m. and 7:00 a.m. Don't worry if people are used to messaging you during those hours. They'll quickly adapt to your new routine, and as a bonus, they might start to look forward to the flurry of messages you send out in the morning.

Another way to take a #TextTimeout is by silencing messages during certain times of the day or while doing specific tasks. For example, I'll silence messages during the time I have set aside to write this book. Every little bing totally distracts me, and I lose my train of thought. I'm sure you can relate. So setting a specific time each day or each week for your #TextTimeout is a good way start getting comfortable with less texting overall.

One final way to take a #TextTimeout is to go big and do what is basically a text detox for a day or two. If you want to try it, be sure to plan ahead—for example, make sure there won't be any urgent messages you'll feel compelled to answer. Then take a day without any messages at all. The goal here is to just reflect on what this experience feels like. Maybe you feel weird, or lonely, or anxious. Just take this short time to be mindful—to experience your emotions instead of always trying to push them away by using your smartphone.

Finally, if you feel like frequent notifications are still a problem even when implementing #TextTimeouts, change the alert settings in your phone so messages only alert you a single time. This small change cuts smartphone notification distractions in half if you currently have alerts set to notify you twice per message, and it can help you stay a bit more present even with lots of messages.

Take Social Media Timeouts

In our modern world, most of us *need* to use technology, *How could we even function without our phone and computer?* we might ask. Indeed, we might need technology for work, coordinating, and other practical uses, but the majority of us actually *don't* need social media. And that's a good thing because research shows that the more we use social media, the more FOMO we experience (Przybylski et al. 2013) and the worse our well-being is likely to be (Tromholt 2016). So a #SocialMediaTimeout may be exactly what we need to jumpstart our happiness.

It may seem hard at first to take a #SocialMediaTimeout—maybe we spend hours on social media every day; maybe it is the first thing we turn to when we wake up and the last thing we see at night. But if this sounds like you, then it is even more important to take occasional breaks to reconnect with yourself and the present moment.

My first #SocialMediaTimeout lasted three years, and it felt great. But admittedly, this was a long time ago before social media was so pervasive. I doubt I could do it again. Besides, there are some good things about social media—we often rely on it for communicating with old friends, distant family, or people with shared interests. So I'm not advocating that you give up social media altogether (unless that's what you want). Instead, I'm suggesting that you take small, intentional breaks from social media to help yourself better understand the impacts it's having on you, short-circuit addictive behaviors, and make the changes that can increase your happiness.

Before starting your #SocialMediaTimeout, decide on a time that you'll do it. Choose a start date and end date, and be sure that the length of time you plan for your #SocialMediaTimeout seems doable *for you*. If you need to, just plan to take a social media break for one day. If you feel up for it, try to take a full week off for your first social media break. Just set a goal that you feel you can achieve and stick to it!

Once you have your #SocialMediaTimeout planned, make an announcement on your social media to let your friends, family, and community know that you're taking a #SocialMediaTimeout. By telling your social media community about your plans, you'll be more likely to reach your goal. This simple little motivation trick helps because it increases accountability—you'll feel more inclined to do what you said you were going to do because you've told other people about it.

Next, get yourself ready for your #SocialMediaTimeout by deleting social media from your phone—yes, delete it entirely. So much of what we do on our phone is automatic—we don't even realize we've picked up our phone and have been scrolling for twenty minutes until something jars us from this smartphone-induced hypnotic state. So you can't trust yourself and rely on willpower alone. Human willpower is a limited resource, so we have to be more strategic.

Delete your social media from your smartphone for your #SocialMediaTimeout. You can always add it back in when you're done. But by not having social media on your phone, you won't have to rely on your willpower to stop you. Instead you'll have a bigger barrier (redownloading the app) that will help you stick to your goals more easily. You might even discover during your #SocialMediaTimeout that you're happier without social media on your phone and decide to ditch it permanently. I did, and I don't miss it at all.

If you use social media on your computer, be sure to log out before you start your #SocialMediaTimeout. You'd be surprised how easy it is to be cruising online and suddenly realize you've ended up on social media—*Whawha! Where am I? And how did I get here?* Whether you mindlessly wandered to social media during a moment of weakness or clicked on a link that took you to social media without you intending to go there, keeping yourself logged out creates a barrier that prevents you from accidentally ending up on social media. And if you end up at the login page, choose to say no, just for this short #SocialMediaTimeout.

One of the benefits of taking a #SocialMediaTimeout, especially if you're an avid social media user, is that you are forced to spend more time with yourself. So take this opportunity to reflect on how you feel and any insights that emerge. While doing your #SocialMediaTimeout, ask yourself these questions to try to better understand your relationship with social media and how it affects your happiness. Then write your answers in your notebook.

- Do you feel any negative emotions when you can't use social media? If so, how come?

- Does not using social media make you feel better? If so, in what ways?

Keep in mind that social media has more negative effects for some people than others. So taking social media breaks will affect each of us differently. Most likely, you'll feel both good and bad during your #SocialMediaTimeout. It can sometimes almost feel like detoxing from an addiction—it feels good to be in control and free from something that feels bad. But it's also kind of scary to be without our crutch—the thing we we're using to distract ourselves from all the other challenges in our lives.

After your #SocialMediaTimeout, decide what you'll do next. Do you want to continue your social media use as before, or would you like to make some changes that might help you be more present in the moment and happier in the long run? Just be sure you're being honest with yourself about what's best for your happiness.

If you decide to add social media back on your phone, try to use this experience as a reset for how you use social media. For example, you can move all your social media apps to the second or third screen, preferably in a folder or somewhere else hidden and hard to get to. And be sure to turn off all notifications to reduce your usage of social media. You might also want to change the color settings on your phone to grayscale (instead of full color), which can lead you to use your apps less because they look less exciting.

Make No-Phone Zones

If you're old enough, you remember when phones were attached to the wall by a cord. There was no taking them with us to the bathroom, on errands, or on vacation. What about now? Is your phone invited with you *everywhere* you go? Most people would say, "Yes!" We seem to have unconsciously slipped into a habit of bringing our phone with us everywhere. *We need it in case of an emergency*, we tell ourselves. This may be true at times, but it's also a bit of an excuse. How often do we *really* have an emergency?

On a snowy day, many years ago before I got my cell phone, my car slid on a patch of ice and got a flat tire. Sure, having a phone to call for help would have been nice, but it was just as easy to flag down a car and ask to make a call on someone else's phone. So first and foremost, remind yourself that it's not the end of the world to not have a phone on you at all times. Life *will* go on.

Next, decide on at least one time each day or week when you'll be #PhoneFree (for example when you run errands, when you're using the bathroom, or when you're exercising). Again, you may want to let your friends, family, and community know that you'll be #PhoneFree before starting this time so they know what to expect of you. Personally, I don't take my phone on errands—errands like grocery shopping, going to the post office, or picking up takeout. Even a small chunk of phone-free time forces us to be with ourselves, which we have to admit, we're kind of afraid to do now.

Next, create #NoPhoneZones, places where your phone is not invited (such as the bedroom, bathroom, or dining room). The goal is to get back more time that will be uninterrupted or disturbed by your phone. It's up to you which #NoPhoneZones you choose. I choose to keep my phone out of the bedroom because it can be harmful to your sleep (not to mention your sex life) to have notifications binging all night long.

Do a Reconnection Retreat

In addition to taking short breaks from specific technologies, it's often also helpful to periodically take more substantial and intentional breaks from technology by doing what I call a #ReconnectionRetreat. This is where you don't use any technology—no phones, TVs, tablets, or computers—and instead actively spend this time reconnecting with everything else in your life that has been neglected—for example, your health, your body, your relationships, your dreams, your passions, your creativity, your community, and your planet.

Usually a #ReconnectionRetreat is a week long (or a weekend) because that's the period of time that most people can fit into their schedules. And although you could try to do your #ReconnectionRetreat at home, it'll likely be harder to disconnect from technology when it's all around you *and* harder to reconnect with everything else when you're in the same environment that contributed to your technology habits in the first place. So the further away from technology you can be, the easier it will be. It's basically like going cold turkey from smoking and drinking—the further away you are from temptation, the better. So go out of town, preferably to a place with little technology, like nature, a developing country, or a remote town.

Keep in mind that this time is not just about disconnecting from technology—it's about reconnecting with the things that'll help you thrive. So do something active with your mind and body because unhappiness in the technology age is driven by an imbalance between overconnecting with technology and underconnecting to other important things. To correct this imbalance, you could attend a wellness workshop, roast marshmallows over an open fire with friends, or go on a yoga retreat. Plan out whatever activities you believe will be most helpful for you.

Having tried a #ReconnectionRetreat myself, I can't overstate how positive the effects are. I spent a week in Mexico with my mom with no phones, Internet, TV, or radio. It was just us, the ocean, conversation, and time. When I got home, I realized that I had lost this buzzing stress that I didn't even realize I had. My brain started working better, and it was easier to get work done. I just felt more like myself somehow. Without all the distractions, I had reconnected to what really mattered. You too can have this experience.

PRACTICE BEING MORE MINDFUL

Let's face it; we spend so much time on our phones or computers that we have few spare moments left to just be. So in addition to taking #TechnologyTimeouts, we also need to relearn how to be mindfully present in these new uninterrupted moments that we now have. By doing so, we can experience our lives more fully and stop feeling like zombies moving aimlessly through life.

When we learn to be more mindful, we are really learning how to pay attention—to personal experiences but also to what's going on with other people, communities, and society at large. When we start paying attention—I mean *really* paying attention—we start to see and experience all sorts of things we've been ignoring, either intentionally or unintentionally. For some of us, this can mean we discover our unconditional love for our romantic partner, that our hobby gives us true joy, or that eating fruits and veggies makes us feel more energetic. But mindfulness does not always result in positive experiences initially. It can also lead us to uncover crushing guilt from having betrayed someone we love, deep rage about a culture that looked the other way when we were assaulted, or overwhelming sadness about the suffering of those in our community or country.

When we become more mindful, both the darkest and brightest parts of our world come roaring into view. Of course, it's easier to appreciate the good things than deal with bad things, but it is incredibly important to our happiness do both. Because when we become mindfully present in our lives, we finally start to feel, well…alive. All the tiny delights of simply being human become crystal clear. All those buried negative emotions bubble to the surface where they can finally be dealt with, perhaps for the very first time. And our increased awareness of the experiences of others can lead us to live more value-driven, purposeful lives. The result? An abundance of happiness, joy, and feelings of connectedness.

Create Mindful Moments

In our technology-crazed world, it's especially hard to develop mindfulness skills. For example, if I go out to eat with a friend, it is almost painful sitting alone at the table waiting for them to come back from the bathroom. This seemingly innocuous experience provokes a surprising amount of anxiety, anxiety that is so easily abated by pulling out my smartphone.

We mindlessly reach for our phones instead of asking ourselves: Why is it that being alone with ourselves is so uncomfortable? As a result, we remain blissfully unaware of whatever it is that's causing our discomfort. And if we don't know what it is, we can't fix it.

As an experiment for this book, I decided that I would no longer pull out my phone when alone at a restaurant, bar, or other social event. Instead, I'd have a mindful moment. I'd just sit there, feel my emotions, and let my thoughts come and go as they desired.

At first, these mindful moments were intense. *This sucks! How long will I sit here with nothing to distract me? Maybe I should just pull out my phone. What harm could it do?* I thought. It was amazing how strong the urge was to just abandon my mindful moments and distract myself with technology. But each time I engaged in a mindful moment, there was less anxiety than the previous time. My emotions would come, and eventually, they would go. And as the intensity of the emotions faded, I was able to pay more attention to what was actually going on inside me.

One time I was sitting alone at the bar having a mindful moment, waiting for my drinking partner to return, and I discovered something I didn't know about myself. I thought: *I feel nervous that a stranger will come up and talk to me. That wouldn't feel safe. If I'm on my phone, no one will try to approach me.* I suddenly realized that because I am a woman, being alone in a public setting *often* feels unsafe. My smartphone made me feel safe! It's no wonder I wanted to be on it. It turned out that I was constructing an imaginary wall around myself while simultaneously distracting myself from my negative feelings.

If you're compelled to pull out your smartphone in certain situations, there is likely some negative emotion that you too are hiding from. And as a result of using your phone, you're unable to uncover, accept, and resolve those feelings. By taking mindful moments, you can start to uncover some of the causes that lead you to overuse your phone. And as a result, it'll be easier to stop using it when you want to.

Decide When to Have Your Mindful Moments

It's time for you to create some mindful moments—moments that are just about being present and paying attention to what's actually happening around you instead of what's happening on a screen. First, decide on a time when you want to have your #MindfulMoments. This could be in the morning, in the evening, during your commute, during meals, or in a specific situation, like when you are waiting for others to arrive at a restaurant or waiting in line for your morning coffee. If you'd like to challenge yourself, choose the time when you *least* want to have a mindful moment because that's when you probably need a mindful moment the most.

What to Do During Your Mindful Moments

Is mindfulness just sitting there in silence and not doing other more fun and entertaining things? Luckily, no, because I downright hate sitting still for long periods of time. Mindfulness is really just a state of being. All it requires is that you maintain a sense of awareness, openness, and acceptance as you go about doing whatever it is that you're doing. It does not necessarily require meditation, a room filled with scented candles, or any other prop.

Even though mindfulness is theoretically possible to practice anywhere, that doesn't mean it comes easy—it didn't for me. On my first attempts, I questioned it relentlessly: *What do you mean be open and aware? What else would I be?!* It wasn't until later that I discovered *how* to be fully aware, open, and accepting, and how important this is for happiness in the technology age. Here's how to get started.

Awareness. To be more aware, try to explore the causes and consequences of your emotions, thoughts, and behaviors. For example, if you are angry at someone, is it actually because of what they did? Or is it because of how they did it, why they did it, how it made you feel, or something in your past that has basically nothing to do with them? By becoming more aware of what's *really* causing your thoughts and emotions, you can better take the right actions to change them.

Openness. To be more open, try not to push away unpleasant thoughts or emotions that arise in mindful moments. For example, many of us listen politely when friends share their struggles, but really, all we want is to end *our own* discomfort of having to be with them while they experience these emotions. Instead, try to open yourself to any and all emotions that arise in you, even if those emotions are unpleasant.

Acceptance. To be more accepting, try to stop judging or censoring your feelings and thoughts. You may have heard judgy statements like "Boys don't cry" or "You're too sensitive" or "Get over it," and it is likely that you will continue to hear these things. We've internalized these messages, so it can be really hard to be accepting of emotions. We usually have to make an active effort not to judge by reminding ourselves that emotions are a natural, useful, and normal experience for all humans.

Do a Quick Mindfulness Practice

Let's try a bit of mindfulness right now. To start, try to create some negative emotions in yourself. An easy way to do this is to watch a movie or online video clip with a sad or emotional scene. Or if you'd like to challenge yourself, you could imagine something in your own life—for example, failing at something, being embarrassed in front of a crowd, or something else that you know makes you feel bad.

Once you have drummed up some negative emotions, stop thinking about the negative experiences and just sit with these emotions. See if you notice any interesting body sensations, emotional changes, or thoughts. Practice not judging yourself or your experiences. And be careful not to either hold on to the emotions or push them away. Just be with yourself until your thoughts and emotions trail off.

When you are done, reflect on this experience in your notebook. Ask yourself the following questions:

- Did you uncover new levels of awareness, or did you stay at the surface?

- Were you able to stay open to whatever came, or did you try to push anything away?

- Did you find yourself accepting your thoughts and emotions as they were, or did you judge yourself for having them?

- What did you like and dislike about this activity?

Developing mindfulness can take time, so don't worry if you felt weird, or bored, or even nothing at all—that's pretty common. If you finished this activity feeling shaky, upset, or overwhelmed, I'd suggest holding off on using this activity again until you've mastered managing your emotions (in step 4). Trying to do too much too soon can be too overwhelming for some folks.

Take Mindful Photos

Another, less intense way to develop mindfulness is by taking mindful photos on your smartphone. So often we walk through life like zombies—our body is present, but our mind is elsewhere. We're not really paying attention, so we miss the things in life that really matter—the things that give us a sense of meaning or purpose. To better pay attention to those parts of our lives, we can snap photos while truly paying attention to what we see (be sure not to think about who will see the photos or where you'll share them—those thoughts take you out of the present moment) (Diehl, Zauberman, and Barasch 2016).

To try out a mindful photos practice, spend one week taking photographs of all the things that give your life even a little bit of meaning. Don't be too picky. Try to snap a shot of anything you can think of that feels meaningful—people, places, important objects, experiences—really anything. For example, I would take mindful photos of my cat, my partner, the garden down the street from me, the fall leaves crunching under my toes, and my stack of postcards that I regularly send to friends and family. Spend a few minutes each day taking these photos. Or, take these photos as you go about your day, trying to notice all the little things in life that you haven't been noticing. Just do whatever works best for you.

At the end of the week, spend a few minutes looking at all your photos. Scroll through them on your smartphone or computer, reflecting on each one. For each one, ask yourself the following questions and write your answers in your notebook:

- What is in this photograph, and why is it meaningful to me?

- What does it make me think of?

- How does it make me feel?

After completing this activity, take a moment to think about what creates true meaning in *your* life. We can never really know what is the meaning *of* life. But we can discover what creates a sense of meaning *in* our life. Write your thoughts and reflections down in your notebook. When you know what gives your life meaning, hopefully you'll want to spend more of your life doing these things and want to spend less time on your phone.

FINAL THOUGHTS

When you take a break from technology, you give yourself the chance to experience the present moment. In years past, we had more opportunities to do this, but now in the technology age, staying present requires deliberate effort. By using any or all of the strategies in this chapter, you can start to retrain your attention and better focus on the things that really matter and give you joy.

Make Meaningful Connections

The great irony in the age of technology is that we have more ways to connect than ever, yet we have never felt so lonely (Holt-Lunstad, Robles, and Sbarra 2017). That's because technology is hurting both the quality and quantity of our social connections. And having healthy social connections is one of the most important contributors to our well-being (Holt-Lunstad, Robles, and Sbarra 2017). So even as we become more *connected* than ever, we are becoming more *disconnected* in the ways that matter to our happiness (Holt-Lunstad, Robles, and Sbarra 2017).

Many of us now work from home, live alone, and communicate mostly through text (messaging, social media, and email). Because so many of our social connections are now mediated by technology, if we want to increase our happiness, it's now pretty much required that we devote extra time and energy to creating healthy relationships both online and offline. In this chapter, you'll learn how to do all that. You'll develop the skills that can help you strengthen relationships, focus on others, and communicate kindly in the technology age. By learning these skills, you can start to reconnect in the ways that matter most for your happiness.

In this chapter, you'll learn how to:

- strengthen relationships

- focus on others

- communicate kindly in text.

STRENGTHEN RELATIONSHIPS

Although our smartphones are just small rectangular objects in our pockets, they are leading to significant shifts in how we experience and interact with the world. Indeed, greater use of electronic devices has been linked to greater depression (Twenge et al. 2018), lower quality social interactions (Brown, Manago, and Trimble 2016), and worse mood (Kushlev and Heintzelman 2017). So how can we prevent our smartphones from hurting our relationships and our happiness?

Don't Substitute Face-to-Face Interactions for Electronic Interactions

It's human nature to need social connection. We often like to think—or we've been told—that we can use our smartphones to meet this need. But it turns out that using electronic devices to connect *socially* doesn't work very well. Our mood and feelings of social connection are not any better when using electronic devices than when not socializing at all (Kushlev and Heintzelman 2017). Worse, when we use our phones socially, we are more likely to use them habitually— to pick them up and use them without even realizing it (Van Deursen et al. 2015). Because we only have a limited amount of time each day, this can lead us to spend less time with others, which, over time, can drastically and negatively impact the quality of our lives.

In fact, it appears that the biggest reason smartphones are harmful to our happiness is because of how they impact our social relationships (Kawachi and Berkman 2001). Social relationships are often easier to build and maintain in person, at least in part because of all the social cues, social norms, and body language that goes along with them. Perhaps it is not surprising then that engaging in in-person social interactions is related to positive outcomes like improved mood (Kushlev and Heintzelman 2017) and less depression. In fact, pretty much all activities that get us around other people—things like attending religious services or engaging in sports—have positive effects on our mental health (Twenge et al. 2018). Conversely, the fewer in-person interactions we have, the more likely it is that our happiness will suffer.

Unfortunately, the convenience of the smartphone has made it easier for us to pass up these in-person social interactions. Most of us *don't* intentionally use our phones to avoid interacting with others; we use our phones because they're easy. We may be less inclined to meet up with a friend in person when we can just text them. We may just peruse our friends' social media pages instead of asking them how they're doing. We may opt to stream a movie instead of going to the theater with friends. But we should not so easily substitute electronic interactions for the real thing. This is exactly how our smartphones outsmart us, because the fewer in-person interactions we have, the more we depend on our phone, leading us to further withdraw—a perpetual downward spiral into the smartphone abyss.

But all hope is not lost for our phones. If you want to use your smartphone for social connection, you can. Instead of engaging in solo activities, like social media, opt instead to do something that involves active participation of others. Electronic interactions *can* be beneficial—particularly when in-person interactions are not possible (Guillory et al. 2015). For example, when you are traveling for work or a close friend has moved out of state, reach out to chat (Desjarlais and Willoughby 2010), video, or play games with people you can't see in person—just be sure to not to sacrifice in-person interactions for these electronic interactions.

Don't Phubb (Phone-Snub) Your Friends

More than half of Americans say that smartphones have made it harder to give others their undivided attention (Kushlev 2018). Just having a smartphone present on a table while engaging in a meaningful conversation can have negative effects, including less empathy, less trust, and interactions that are not as meaningful or satisfying (Brown, Manago, and Trimble 2016; Przybylski and Weinstein 2013). We kind of know this intuitively; the majority of us believe that when someone pulls out their smartphone, phone snubbing or #Phubbing us, it hurts the conversation (Rainie 2015). Maybe we feel annoyed, or ignored, or disrespected. Oddly, we seem to forget that when we phubb others, it has the same effect on them. And we don't even realize that using our smartphones during social events actually diminishes our *own* experience of those events too—we enjoy these experiences less and get bored more easily (Dwyer, Kushlev, and Dunn 2017). So we continue to blindly use our smartphones, believing that everyone, except us, is responsible for our unsatisfying social interactions.

So what can we do to improve our social interactions? One answer: don't use your phone when with others. But that's easier said than done, right? How does this work IRL, when you've got the constant buzzing of notifications constantly interrupting you? Here are some simple guidelines for how to use your phone wisely when with others.

First, turn off notifications for everything that is nonessential. For example, on my phone, I only keep notifications on for phone calls and text messages. There will never be a social media post or app notification important enough that I would allow it to pull me away from connecting with others. You might be different, so you'll have to decide for yourself where you draw the line. But you do need to draw a line *somewhere*. So go into your phone right now and turn off all notifications that are nonessential *for you*.

Second, define for yourself what you consider to be an important call or text. What if you are waiting to hear back from someone who needs directions? What if your boss is planning to get back to you about an important project? What if the babysitter needs to be able to get in touch with you quickly? This is real life, and there are real situations that will prevent you from being #PhoneFree 100 percent of the time.

Take a moment now to write down the types of messages you would consider to be "important" in your notebook. If you find that your list is getting really long, then zoom in on what's "extremely important."

My response might look like this:

Important messages to me are any from my partner (because he texts when we're working out plans) and if I'm waiting to hear back about something important for work. Pretty much no other messages are urgently important.

Before meeting up with others, use your list to determine how your phone will or will not be part of the interaction. If you're expecting an important message, leave your phone on. If you're not, turn your phone off or keep it in a separate location.

Third, there will be times—maybe many times—when you decide to keep your phone on. So what do you do then? How do you keep it from hurting your interactions? Your underlying goal here will be to devote 100 percent of your attention to others when you are with them and 100 percent of your attention to your phone when you are with it. I have found the best way to do this is to periodically excuse myself and only take my phone out when I am some place private, like the bathroom or outside.

One fun way to help you keep your phone away when with others is to make it a game. Your goal in the #InvisiblePhoneGame is to never let other people *see* or *hear* your phone. That doesn't mean you can't be on your phone—it just means it should be invisible to others. Here's how you play: If you feel a buzz and pull out your phone, even if just to check for a second, you get a point. If you answer a text in front of others, you get a point. If your phone rings and others hear it, you get a point. Count up your points each day and see if you can lower your score the next day.

Want to improve even faster? Ask your friends and family to help you. We are so used to pulling out our phones for just about everything. Some estimates say we reach for our phones an average of 150 times per day. So we might not even notice when we do it. By asking others to keep you accountable, you may be able to outsmart your smartphone more easily and quickly.

Fourth, decide what you will give your attention to. So you've stepped away from others to check your phone. Maybe you see a text from your babysitter—your kiddo has a slight cough but nothing to worry about. Maybe your boss emailed you feedback on a project, but it doesn't need to be reviewed until Monday. In these moments, keep in mind your list of important messages. If this message is not important, don't engage with it, because if you *do* engage with it, your attention could get hijacked—not just in *that* moment, but for *many moments* afterward, for as long as it takes for your brain to refocus on what's happening in front of you.

For example, let's say I decide to read my boss's email, and I discover that instead of positive feedback, I get a list of things I need to fix. Once I've read the message, even if I don't plan to respond, that's all I can think about for the next hour. In this example, reading that message prevents me from being able to pay attention and be fully present during any of my interactions not just in that minute, but for a *full hour*. So instead of reading or listening to every message right when you get it, ask yourself: "Is this message important enough that I'm willing to risk it ruining the next few minutes, or hours, or however long it'll take me to focus again?" If so, then fine. We each have to decide what we will and will not allow in our own lives. But if you do decide to read the message anyway, reflect on how it makes you feel during subsequent conversations. Ask yourself:

- Are you having a hard time listening?
- Does your mind keep going back to the message?
- Would you make the same decision next time?

If your mind is elsewhere, then your interactions will end up being less satisfying for you and for others. That's why following each of these guidelines can really help you enjoy your social interactions more. And, as a pleasant side effect, you may notice that your efforts start to have positive effects on others as well. These days, we tend to be accustomed to low-quality interactions, constantly interrupted by buzzes and people staring at screens while only half-listening to us. So when we start giving people *our* undivided attention, they really appreciate it and often engage more fully with us in return.

Since I personally started following these guidelines, all my social interactions have improved immensely—people seem more eager to talk to me, I am more often invited to social events, and people even try harder to keep their phones out of view when they are with me. I'm not sure if they realize they are doing it—I think it's just human nature to treat others as they treat you. And since I don't phubb them, leaving them feeling neglected, they try not to phubb me. So putting our phones away when with others can lead to an upward spiral of positive interactions.

Try Casual Connecting

After spending the last few decades hearing, "Don't talk to strangers," I wouldn't be surprised if you felt a bit anxious about walking up to random people and talking to them. Someone asked me for directions the other day, and it caught me by surprise. *Why don't they just use their phone?* I thought. But it turns out that even seemingly trivial interactions with strangers—like asking someone for directions or chatting with the barista or cashier—help us feel more socially connected (Sandstrom and Dunn 2014; Kushlev, Proulx, and Dunn 2017).

Unfortunately, carrying our smartphone with us often results in us missing out on these opportunities to casually connect with others. We rarely just accidentally fall into conversations with strangers anymore. As a result, we can start to feel like we don't have a sense of community, but we can't figure out why. A great way to start undoing our feelings of disconnection is through #CasualConnection. And we don't need to get rid of our phone to do it. We just need to talk to strangers.

Take a moment now to think of situations when you could have a #CasualConnection—a brief or longer conversation with someone you don't already know. Could you share a few words with someone on the subway or bus instead of playing on your phone? What about saying hello to the people who pass by you on the street? Next time you see a familiar neighbor, might you stop to get to know them a bit better? Write down as many #CasualConnection ideas as you can in your notebook.

Next, write a list of the actual words you could say: *I like your shoes. Nice weather we're having. How about that sports team?* Sometimes it can be hard to figure out what to say in the moment, so brainstorming a bunch of ideas ahead of time, whether or not you choose to use them, can make it a bit easier to connect when opportunities arise. I mean, let's face it; it can be a little uncomfortable to chat with some random stranger, so whatever you can do to make it easier for yourself is helpful.

With your list completed, start by choosing one situation where you'll put away your phone and have a #CasualConnection instead. The situation I first chose was at the grocery store. Every week when I shop, I have at least one brief interaction with a stranger. Often I'll comment on what a great price something is to a fellow customer, or I'll chat with the butcher while he wraps up something for me. And because there are long lines at my local grocery store, sometimes I'll start up a conversation with whoever is in line with me. I know these tiny interactions seem small and irrelevant, but they actually do have a real positive impact on happiness and are especially important now in the technology age.

FOCUS ON OTHERS

Another way smartphones can hurt our relationships is through social media and its tendency to heighten our self-focus. For example, we use social media to express *our* opinions. We collect images that *we* like. We share *our* accomplishments. This is how social media focuses your attention on how *you* feel, think, and behave (Ingram 1990) on what *you* are doing, what *you* are like, and what *your* beliefs or attitudes are.

Being self-focused isn't inherently a bad thing. In individualistic cultures (like in America), we value our freedom to be independent, separate, distinctive human beings. So we want to know who we are and what we feel, and knowing these things about ourselves is crucial for our identities. But heightened self-focus has a downside. When you regularly focus on yourself, you'll notice any dissatisfaction, anxiety, or general malaise that you might not have otherwise noticed. And bringing your attention to these negative emotions amplifies them (Ingram 1990). For example, if you're like me, you might ask yourself, "Am I happy?" By focusing on yourself, you realize that you're not as happy as you want to be and maybe spend the rest of the day feeling sorry for yourself. This is how excess self-focus reduces happiness instead of increasing it. And this is why, despite everything you may have heard in self-help books or articles, spending tons of time focusing on yourself and your happiness tends to backfire.

So what *do* you do instead? The answer is: focus on others. When we focus on other people, especially their happiness, we counter intuitively increase *our own* positive emotions too (Boehm and Lyubomirsky 2009). Plus, we build a more enduring sense of happiness than if we had just focused on increasing our own happiness.

Maybe you decide that you want to use social media despite its tendency to cause self-focus. That's okay. You just have to be sure you're engaging with social media in ways that focus your attention outward and not on yourself. Here's some ways to do it.

Learn How to Create Prosocial Posts

When we "share" a post on social media about our new car, our amazing vacation, our new job, or whatever it is that we have, we are really just "humble bragging." For example, I might "share" a cool thing I did, a pretty meal I ate, or a fun party I went to—all things that I *didn't* actually share with you. As a result, we induce feelings of envy and resentment in the very people we hope to connect with. And unfortunately, that envy doesn't go away once they scroll past your post. It is felt deeply and can lead these people to feel less close to you in the future. So these types of posts can inadvertently harm our relationships IRL (Verduyn et al. 2017).

To strengthen social connections, instead of harming them, we need to write #ProsocialPosts. Prosocial behavior is any behavior intended to promote friendship, connection, or helpfulness. A #ProsocialPost is just a post intended for the same purpose. We might post something helpful, kind, supportive, or generous—anything that supports and strengthens the relationships we have online. Here are some guidelines for getting started.

First, keep your eyes open for ways to be supportive of others. For example, if a friend is struggling with something, you could share advice or words of support. If a friend is about to start a new job, you could wish them luck. Or, you could give a compliment when someone posts a picture of themselves. You can take this practice one step further by calling them to talk IRL instead of posting. By doing so, you're telling that person, "Hey, I care about you."

Second, create your own "giving posts" or messages. You could randomly say a kind word to a friend you haven't talked to in a long time, remind them about an experience you had with them that you are grateful for, or share a cute video or image with someone who you think would like it. All you need to do to create a successful #ProsocialPost is pay attention to what each person cares about. You started building this skill in step two, but now it's time to use this skill again by staying present and noticing the things that matter to the people who matter to you.

For example, one of my friends is really into weird garden plants. So whenever I see something related to cool gardens—like a giant tomato plant tree—I share it with her. Another friend of mine has tons of photos of my social group from high school. Rather than posting selfies, she shares these old photos of all of us, reminding us of the good memories we created together. Another friend almost exclusively shares jokes. I always know that his posts are going to give me a giggle, which I really appreciate. To create good #ProsocialPosts, all you need to remember is that your posts should benefit others rather than yourself. Don't forget to tag these posts with #ProsocialPost to help your network get familiar with idea and hopefully spread it so they start sharing prosocial posts with you too.

Lastly, let people know that you appreciate when they share #ProsocialPosts—"like" the news articles, funny videos, or images that you enjoyed. By saying "thanks" to the people who share #ProsocialPosts, you're letting them know that those kinds of posts are valued, and this encourages them to post like this more often. Who knows, maybe your entire network will shift, and everyone will benefit more from the time they spend on social media. That's certainly what I hope for.

Try Out Causal Kindness

Are you hurling insults at anyone that you disagree with, find offensive, or don't understand fully? Or are you choosing to be kind, even when the person on the other side of the screen has been unkind to you? The truth is that we have to choose whether we want to respond to anger with anger, hate with hate, or instead respond to the ugliness on the Internet by being thoughtful, kind, and considerate. Kindness is clearly the harder option, but it also the option that is better for our happiness.

I'll be the first to admit that handling online negativity can be challenging. I've written hundreds of articles online about how to increase happiness. Despite this positive topic, I still get comments that criticize, insult, and are unkind. Indeed, the Internet has become an outlet for our worst impulses. Being on the receiving end of cyberbullying, or even witnessing it, can hurt, make us angry, and lead us to seek revenge.

But in the long run, telling someone how wrong, stupid, or lame they are helps no one. If anything, it might lead them to treat people even worse online, and we have to admit it, being a jerk makes us feel worse too. Even though we might feel vindicated in standing up for ourselves, in standing up for others, or for expressing our point of view, we've just generated negative emotions for ourselves and everyone else who sees what we've written. If we keep up this negative cycle, we're all headed to a really dark place—a place where kindness, compassion, and consideration no longer exist. So we have to start responding to online negativity in more positive and effective ways.

Think of Your Comments as Acts of Kindness

When you read a nasty comment online, instead of appeasing your desire to be right, to change others, or to shame others for their comments, remember to think of your comments in terms of what they can do for the person receiving them. Remember to post #ProsocialPosts even when the person doesn't appear to deserve it. When your goal is to give the other person a gift that helps them, your comments become acts of kindness instead of retaliations of hate. As a result, you likely feel more connected to others and they'll feel more connected to you.

Is it hard to practice random acts of kindness in response to comments that evoke negative emotions in you? Of course it is! That's why online discussions so easily go off the rails. But the truth is that it's up to us to change the dynamic. Here's how to do it.

Question your assumptions. It's natural for us to think we understand why someone is acting a certain way. We see their actions and make assumptions about who they are and how they think based only this tiny bit of information. This can lead *us* to be the ones who treat people unfairly and unkindly because we don't understand their experience and motivations. For example, maybe someone says something negative about one of our political beliefs. We think it's because they are a jerk, but maybe it's just because they believe a different approach would be the most helpful and kind. They see things differently than we do.

Lead with questions and curiosity. Before jumping to conclusions, ask questions to learn about the situation better. Yelling at people is certainly not going to make them change their mind or be any less of a bully. Instead, ask them questions like: *It sounds like you see this situation differently. Can you share your perspective with me so I can better understand where you're coming from?*

Clarify the value of your feedback. If others are open to answering your questions, you will likely better understand the causes of their actions and can respond more effectively. To be sure your responses are kind, make sure you can clearly articulate why the response you are giving is useful to the person. It probably would be helpful to say something like: *I want to make sure we both understand each other's perspectives, so can I tell you why I feel the way I do?* By creating an environment where people can share their opinions honestly and listen to each other, a lot of negativity can be overcome.

Use Kindness as the Antidote to Unkindness

Does this rational, kind, considerate approach always work? If the person's objective is to hurt you, get a rise out of you, or discredit you, you might need to try other techniques to build bridges online. Here are some suggestions:

Don't give them what they want. When you see other people being trolled, don't respond to the troll, yell at the troll, or give the troll any attention whatsoever.

Use trolling as a reminder to be kind to the person being trolled. Undo the negative comments of the troll by supporting the person being trolled. Write a kind, caring, or complimentary message to support them or what they've shared online.

Offer a random act of kindness to the troll in a private message. No one is hateful or harmful to others unless they have also been harmed in some way. Remember, each of our brains evolved based on our personal experiences, and everyone has a reason for acting the way they do. So consider reaching out with kindness; they probably need it more than you realize.

With these tools in your toolbox, you can use cyberbullying and trolling as opportunities to practice kindness. As a result, you can start to build happiness and connection.

Be Prosocial Anytime

You don't have to wait for a friend to post or a bully to say something mean to be prosocial. You can do this anytime. For example, you could leave a kind note on a blog post you liked or compliment some-one's photo, article, or video just about anywhere on the Internet.

Take a moment now to brainstorm a list of #ProsocialPosts you could give to strangers online and write your ideas down in your notebook.

Now give one a try. Make your first #ProsocialPost. Then ask yourself:

- How did it make you feel? Good? Bad?

- How could you make it feel better in the future?

- Might you prefer one type of #ProsocialPost over another type?

Note down your answers in your notebook. Then, schedule a time in your calendar to do something that makes you feel connected each week. Set yourself a reminder or alarm so you don't forget. Be sure it's a time when you'll have a few moments—for example, I have my reminder set for Sunday when I don't have much to do. As a bonus, by spreading your actions out across time, you increase and extend their impact.

COMMUNICATE KINDLY IN TEXT

It used to be easier to tell when we made people angry or sad or excited. We'd see their faces rise or fall and know when the things we said were helpful or hurtful. So we could take the necessary steps to make sure our relationship wasn't harmed. Now, we mostly communicate with text. Emails are short; text messages are even shorter. We often rely on truncated, dashed-off text messages to maintain our personal relation-ships. We have no facial expressions or tone of voice or conversation to give us more information. A smiley face or series of exclamation points can help assure us that the text is meant to express positive emotion, but texts do not always include these extra emotion indica-tors. Our friends' busy schedules lead to abrupt messages; our partner's playful sarcasm isn't always read as playful. Yet, interpreting and responding to these text messages effectively is now a requirement for maintaining healthy relationships, and therefore, also our happiness. So we need to build some skills here.

Put Yourself in the Texter's Shoes

No two people see emotions in the same way. We have different points of view that lead us to draw different conclusions based on the same information. For example, if Bob wrote: "My wife missed our ten-year anniversary," one person might think he is angry, while another person might think he is sad. This is because we interpret emotions through our own emotional lens. We ask ourselves, "How would *I* feel in this situation?" Then we make the mistake of thinking everyone else would feel the same way we would.

In reality, we *don't* tend to feel the same way about the same things. So we are really bad at figuring out how other people feel. And the less we have to go off of, the harder it is. If a text reads, "I love this wonderful kitten," we can easily conclude that this text is expressing positive emotions. If a text reads, "I hate this hard work," that seems pretty negative. But, if a text reads, "This wonderful kitten is hard work," what emotion is being expressed?

One approach to detecting emotions when they appear to be mixed is to use the *bag-of-words* method. This just means that we evaluate each word for how positive and negative we think it is. So we'd think about the words in this text: wonderful, kitten, hard, work. How positive are the words "kitten" and "wonderful"? And how negative are the words "hard" and "work"? By looking at how positive *and* negative each word is, you may be able to figure out the predominant emotion the texter is trying to express.

Now let's imagine that we get a text that is pretty clearly negative—something like, "You were a real jerk at dinner last night!" You might think, *That's easy; this person is clearly angry.* That may be true, but it's not the whole truth. It turns out that we rarely experience negative emotions on their own. Rather, when we experience a negative emotion, like anger, we tend to experience all the other negative emotions too, like sadness and fear (Posner, Russel, and Peterson 2005). One negative emotion may be stronger than others in any given circumstance, but they almost always rise and fall together.

So when you get a text that you're pretty certain expresses anger, you can be almost certain that this person is also feeling at least a little bit sad and fearful, regardless of whether they are expressing it or not. Keeping this in mind can help you respond to challenging texts in more effective ways. Rather than firing back with your own anger, you're better off exploring how the other person *really* feels.

Remember the earlier example where Bob's wife missed their ten-year anniversary? What if you asked Bob to tell you more? Bob might tell you that his wife died, and that is why she missed their anniversary. Suddenly, we understand that Bob is feeling sadness more than anger. Or, Bob might tell you that his wife blew him off to do something else. Then we'd understand that Bob is likely feeling more angry than sad. Next time you are unsure about how someone feels, just ask for more info. By doing so, you focus on their feelings, and not so much on your feelings about their feelings. And you have a better chance of keeping the relationship healthy.

FINAL THOUGHTS

In the technology age, we must work harder to sustain healthy social connections. Hopefully, this chapter helped you get a bit clearer how to do this. And with these skills in your toolbox, you are now more prepared to start a more challenging task: managing your emotions. By learning to better manage emotions, you'll have more control over your behavior, and as a result, you'll be better able to outsmart your smartphone.

Manage Your Emotions

In the first three steps, you learned some of the most important skills for building happiness *in the technology age*. That's why these steps are key when learning how to outsmart your smartphone. But science has shown that there are lots of other skills you can build to increase your happiness and improve your life. So which skills should you focus on next?

Answering this question is tricky because most researchers study the benefit of one happiness skill at a time. So it's hard to tell which skills are the *most* important for our happiness. To figure out which skills tend to be the most important right now, in the technology age, I posted a quiz (similar to the quiz you took at the beginning of this book) on my website, http://www.berkeleywellbeing.com (Davis 2016). By analyzing the results of the quiz, I was able to see which skills are most closely linked to happiness.

Three skills stood out as having the strongest links to happiness: self-compassion, positivity, and resilience. Among the thousands of people who took the quiz, the people who had developed these skills tended to be the happiest. This suggests that these skills are essential for happiness in our current technology-crazed world. And that makes sense because when we manage our emotions effectively, we no longer need to rely on our smartphones (or other crutches like alcohol, shopping, or food) to manage our emotions for us. So at this point in the book, we're going to focus on building these three emotion-management skills.

In this chapter, you'll learn how to:

- cultivate self-compassion

- practice positivity

- build resilience.

CULTIVATE SELF-COMPASSION

When we don't feel good about ourselves, it's easy to think that there's something fundamentally wrong with us; it feels deeply rooted and unchangeable. In reality, though, we may have just been repeatedly exposed to messages that told us we weren't good enough. As we discussed earlier in this book, some of these messages come from media, for example the images that remind us that other people are more attractive, smarter, or richer than us. But these messages can also come from the people we care most about—your mother might make a negative comment about your appearance, your father about your career, or your romantic partner about your smarts.

Remember, our brains learn from everything they encounter. And if we hear these messages enough times, regardless of where they come from, we start to believe them. We think, *Maybe I'm not good enough, attractive enough, or smart enough.* And we start to repeat these messages to ourselves—we treat ourselves the same way our world does. To combat our inner self-critic, and the outside ones, we need to build self-compassion by learning how to say, "No more," to these damaging messages. But in this world, where media's damaging messages are everywhere—including in our pocket!—it won't be easy. Cultivating self-compassion in the technology age takes real courage. But I know you're up to the challenge, and I'll help you through it.

Say No to Messages that Harm Your Self-Worth

You wouldn't know it by looking at me—because of my chubby cheeks and round belly—but I eat ridiculously well and exercise regularly. Still, I always felt bad about myself because of my weight. As a result, I've lost hundreds of pounds in my life—twenty pounds on and twenty pounds off, over and over again, ad nauseam. That is until one day, I just got sick of it. It was time to start rewiring my brain to accept myself and my body just as it is. Instead of doing what was easy for me—feeling bad about myself and then dieting until I felt better—I decided to face my fears head on, quit crash dieting, and figure out why it was so hard for me to accept my slightly pudgy self.

Using my mindfulness skills (from step two), I started paying more attention to what, exactly, caused me to feel bad about myself. Was it media? Was it the people in my life? Or was it just inside my own head? While watching TV, especially reality TV, I definitely noticed that I was heavier than most of the people. A pang of embarrassment crept over me. When scrolling through my social media, I saw my friends' selfies, beautiful and Photoshopped to perfection. Pang, a little bit of envy crept over me. But even when talking to my friends, I heard remarks about weight, "I can't eat that. It'll go straight to my thighs," or "She'd look good if she lost twenty pounds." Even though those comments weren't aimed at me, pang, I felt worse about myself.

What I didn't realize, until I really started paying attention, is that yes, media's messages hurt self-worth. But what was more shocking, and angering, is that the messages media creates are so pervasive that they have become a part of us too. We all believe the messages we hear—the messages that we have to be fit, and attractive, and funny, and nice, and well...perfect. And because we *all* have been taught to believe these messages, we spread them to others without out even realizing it. These messages are such an integral part of our culture (at least in America) that our efforts to avoid them are futile. That's why simply giving up our TVs, or social media, or magazines is an incomplete solution.

But wait. All hope is not lost. We can make changes to ourselves that improve our self-worth. When I started really paying attention, it became clear how hard it was going to be not to let these messages affect my thoughts, feelings, and actions. Each time I encountered one of these messages, my anxiety grew. *Just lose the weight and be accepted by society again—stop these negative emotions,* I'd think. But I stuck to my goal. Eventually, I started to notice something shifting in my mind. Instead of believing these negative messages, I started to see myself as strong for fighting them. I started feeling more confident and authentic. The people who wanted me to be something other than who I am started to exit my life. The people who remained made me feel good about myself just as I am. It turns out making the decision to accept myself was the hardest part. Once I did it, the world did too.

What about you? What parts of yourself do you have a hard time accepting? Maybe you feel ugly, or weird, or stupid. Take a moment now to identify your most fragile spots and write them down in your notebook.

Over the next week, pay attention to the messages you hear from media, social media, others, or just in your head that hurt your self-worth. Whenever you notice something has made you feel badly about yourself, pull out your notebook as soon as you can, and write down the answers to these questions:

- What are you feeling?

- What triggered this feeling? Was is text, images, or words that someone said to you?

- How will you refute the message in your head? What will you tell yourself instead?

When we have believed, for so long, that some part of us is bad, it can be hard to believe that we are indeed good. Maybe we have struggled to clarify (and then pursue) exactly what would make us feel like a person we could root for. But by uncovering the unhealthy messages we have believed without question, and choosing to fight these messages courageously, we can more easily be the person that we want to be.

Write Supportive Notes to Yourself

When we are working on accepting ourselves and fighting damaging messages, we may feel weak. So we need to replace damaging messages with supportive ones. To start, write a bunch of notes that say nice things to yourself. For example, you could write, "You rock," or "You can succeed in whatever you put your mind to." Put these notes up around your house, your car, your lock screen on your phone, your computer's screen saver, or anywhere else that you'll see them regularly. This will help you spend more time thinking about these positive messages.

You can also write self-compassionate notes in your notebook. In these notes, imagine that you are talking to yourself like you would talk to a young child. Reassure "this child" that he or she is a valuable, worthwhile, and beautiful human being. Remind the child (which is you) of his or her abilities and good qualities (Neff and Germer 2013). Instead of focusing on all the things wrong with you, focus on what's right. You might try thinking of your quirks as good things because they make you uniquely you. Try to be silly in your notes, reminding yourself your awkward laugh is cute or your inability to remember people's names makes it easier for you to accept when other people forget yours. Remember, it's our humanness, not our perfection, that draws people to us and makes us special.

If you'd like to get even more benefit from these notes, enter them in your phone or calendar and set a daily or weekly notification so your phone automatically sends you these supportive messages. If you use this trick, you'll get your smartphone to start helping you build your happiness.

PRACTICE POSITIVITY

I remember my mom's 1980s beat-up Datsun like I saw it yesterday. The front fender bowed in the middle, like a V, ever since the breaks went out and mom crashed through a wood fence. The drawer in the dashboard was just an empty hole after it was stolen during a break-in for the dollar and change that was in it. The hood was charred from that time the engine caught on fire. That Datsun was a complete disaster…but I still loved it.

Despite being an unreliable piece of crap, that car was the catalyst for so many amazing, unforgettable moments in my life. By leaving us stranded on the side of the road, that car sparked opportunities to spend valuable time with my mom. Because it was so obnoxious, that car gave me material for wacky stories to tell my friends. And because of its unreliability, that car created experiences that made me brave and strong. So even though that car was nothing but trouble, I saw it as a blessing. Somehow, I was able to turn it into something positive.

When you harness the power of positivity, it's amazing the impact it has on your life. It makes every moment worth experiencing and every goal worth shooting for. You just can't help but be optimistic, even when everyone around you is miserable. So how do you start practicing positivity in the technology age?

Build a More Positive Brain

Many people believe that positivity is a personality trait, but it turns out that positivity can be learned. All you need to do is shift the way your brain processes positive information (MacLeod et al. 2002; Wadlinger and Isaacowitz 2008).

In the technology age, we are being trained to focus mostly on the negative. We read sensational headlines in the news, and our social media feeds often highlight the negative posts because these are the posts that get our attention and will keep us online longer. So our brains are trained to focus mostly on the negative—we have strong neural pathways that make it easier for us to pay attention to the negative in situations. By the time we reach adulthood, especially if we watch any amount of news, our brains can find the negative things in just about any situation. These negative neural pathways are mostly permanent. So just telling yourself to "stop" seeing the negative side of things is ridiculously hard. However, we *can* train our brains to create new neural pathways that help us see the positive more easily.

One way to start building a more positive brain is by memorizing lists of positive words. Why? Because when your brain has to memorize something, it connects it to other parts of your brain. The more connected a positive word is to other things in your brain—like other memories, emotions, or thoughts—the more accessible that word, and its concept, will be when you want to use it in daily life (Davis et al. 2013; Siegle, Ghinassi, and Thase 2007). So when you're going about your daily life and your brain forms an opinion about something, the positive words, and any information that's linked to these words in your brain, can come to your mind more quickly. Of course, it takes memorizing lots of positive word lists to retrain your brain. Still, I find this is one of the easiest ways for people to start practicing positivity, especially if positivity is something they struggle with.

Let's try memorizing a few words now. Memorize the list below. Take as long as you need.

Trust, Radiant, Spirit, Satisfied, Desire, Wish, Jewel

Got them memorized? Okay. Set a reminder on your phone to go off sometime later today. When it does, try to recall all the words in the correct order.

To continue building a more positive brain, do this practice daily with a variety of different positive words until you find that these positive words are coming to mind in your daily life. You can search for lists of positive words online or check out my positivity workbook at http://www.berkeleywellbeing.com. As you improve at this, you can challenge yourself by trying to remember even more words at one time, trying to recall the words in reverse order, or trying to remember them for longer periods of time.

Another way to work with these positive words is to print them out on cards, cut them into two pieces, shuffle them all together, and then find each card's match. For example, the word "laughter" would be cut into "laug" and "hter." Your goal is to put all the positive words back together by matching the two-word pieces of each positive word. This practice can help make it easier for your brain to recall positive information when it needs it because your brain has to search through all its memories and information to figure out what the word is. As a result, this activity can help strengthen the neural pathways that generate positivity.

Let's try this activity now. Match the word pieces below to create complete words. List the positive words that you found in your notebook. Example: The underlined words "kind" and "ness" = kindness.

hter	insp	mism	ause
ectful	<u>kind</u>	ired	appl
ected	opti	outst	<u>ness</u>
prot	resp	laug	anding

Create Positive Moments

We sometimes think of happiness as an enduring experience characterized by a sense of meaning, purpose, and joy. In reality, happiness is a collection of many different thoughts, feelings, actions, and experiences, and because our lives are ever-changing, happiness ebbs and flows. If we want our ebbs and flows to stay in a semihappy range, we have to continually generate positive moments that help us pick ourselves back up from a slump and boost our happiness.

We know this intuitively, which is why so many of us turn to our smartphones for a little boost. The problem is that we often seek *pleasure* at the cost of *happiness*. It may feel good in the moment to pop into social media, but we feel worse later, leading to an addictive pursuit of positive moments. Instead of pursuing these fleeting positive moments, let's learn some skills for creating the type of positive moments that actually generate happiness in the longer term.

Generate Positivity Automatically

The first trick to creating positive moments involves tricking your brain into making boring things more positive using what is referred to as classical conditioning. The idea is that when two stimuli are repeatedly paired, the response that was first elicited by the second stimulus is now elicited by the first stimulus alone. For example, for many of us, our favorite food is something that we ate as a child with our families. This happens because the positive feelings of being with family and the particular food got paired in our brain. As a result, we now get the warm-fuzzy feelings that we got from spending time with family just from eating the food alone, even if our family is not currently present.

Classical conditioning is used all the time in advertising. For example, have you ever wondered why "sex sells"? It's because sexy ads provoke positive emotions in us, and our brains end up pairing those emotions with the food, product, or whatever else is being sold. Even though I don't condone the manipulation of our brains to sell products, the lesson is that classical conditioning is a surprisingly powerful strategy that can be used to change our thoughts, emotions, and behaviors. So let's use it to create positive moments that are actually *good* for our happiness.

How do you use classical conditioning to boost your positivity? Well, you just repeatedly link objects—like your computer mouse, your headphones, or even your front door—with positive thoughts and feelings. Pretty soon, these boring objects will generate positivity automatically! That's classical conditioning at work. This trick can help you create positive moments from things that previously had no emotional benefit to you.

Want to try it?

Take a moment now to choose an object that you see every day. Choose something that doesn't make you happy or sad like your shoe, the salt shaker, or a particular mug. Got it? Good. Now, every time you see that object for the next week, take thirty seconds to think about one specific positive experience—for example, maybe a sunny day on the beach, family members, or that one time when you had the most fun ever. But just choose one positive experience.

At the end of the week, look at your object and ask yourself the following questions. Write your answers down in your notebook.

- What does the object make me think of?

- Does the object generate any positive emotions for me?

- Do I feel any bodily sensations (like tingles) when looking at the object?

The effects of this practice can be subtle at first, so it might take longer than a week before the object automatically generates positive moments for you. So just keep at it.

Create Positivity Triggers

Another way to generate small bursts of positivity is by creating positivity triggers. This practice is similar to the previous one except you'll be linking positive moments to a particular time instead of a particular object.

First set an alarm or alert on your phone with its own unique noise or ringtone. A good rule of thumb is to set your alarm for a time when it won't interrupt other important tasks or social events—for example, a good time might be during your commute, a regular break time, or right before a regular meal. This way, you'll be using your smartphone in ways that help you rather than hurt you.

Now, think of one thing that makes you really happy, like your romantic partner, or kittens, or sunsets. Write your one thing down in your notebook.

Every time the alarm goes off, think of this positive thing. Really try to get sucked into the positive feelings and enjoy this positive moment. Do this activity each day for a month.

Just adding this one small positive moment to each day can help keep your happiness elevated. Over time, you may even start to feel these positive emotions at this time of day even if you no longer use the alarm. As a result, you'll have a few more positive moments in your life than you did before.

Practice Gratitude When You're Online

When we express gratitude at work, we can more easily gain the respect and camaraderie of those we work with. When we share our gratitude for our partners or friends, they are more generous and kind to us. When we feel grateful for our day-to-day, we find more meaning and satisfaction with life. Gratitude clearly makes us more positive. But it's not always clear when and how to show our gratitude. In particular, it can feel uncomfortable to share gratitude in person, especially when we're new to gratitude. Luckily, we can use technology to practice gratitude more easily. And by doing so, we make our online time more beneficial to our happiness.

The easiest way to get started with practicing gratitude is with a text or social media message. Take a moment now to write down the names of three people you feel fairly comfortable with. Next to each name, write down at least one thing about each person that you are thankful for. It could be something they did for you. For example, did this person help you figure out what to do about a problem at work? Did they buy you a coffee, drink, or meal recently? Did they say something nice or do something nice for you? Or it could be something about them. For example, are they just generally a kind person? Are they funny? Do they cook really yummy food?

Once you have your list, message each person a sentence or two to share your gratitude. It could be something as simple as, *Hey, you rock! I'm so glad to have you as a friend.* Or it could be more specific: *Remember that time when my car broke down and you picked me up? I just wanted to say thanks!* Try to get in the habit of sending these messages regularly—they'll get you thinking positively. If you have a hard time remembering to do this, set a reminder in your calendar or phone to do this once per week.

To take your gratitude practice up a notch, send a note or letter to someone who you never properly thanked for something important. Your letter could be about anything. Maybe you want to thank a friend for always being there for you. Or maybe you want to thank your romantic partner for a very specific experience, like a date. In your letter, be sure to go beyond just stating the positive ways they make *you* feel and state what you value about *them.* Send this letter to the other person in a message, email, text, or by snail mail.

Practice Gratitude Using Your Smartphone

Not all types of gratitude should be practiced in a public setting like social media. For example, posts or memes that say things like "Grateful to be alive" or #Blessed can actually irk others. To some viewers, these posts come off as sounding trite or Pollyannaish. In addition, posts where we share our gratitude about what *we* have (that others don't have) may actually have negative effects on our relationships because they come off sounding like a humble brag. For example, posts about how grateful we are for an awesome vacation or our loving relationship partner can leave others feeling envious or resentful. It's wonderful if you are grateful for these things, but expressing your gratitude publicly in this way is usually not helpful. Instead of practicing this type of gratitude on social media, opt instead to record it privately.

One way to practice gratitude privately is to write a list of three things you are grateful for today. For example, today I am grateful it's sunny, grateful that I get to spend the evening with good friends, and grateful I'm having a good hair day. Build your gratitude habit by tracking three good things that happened to you each week (Emmons and McCullough 2003). Track these good things in your notebook or on your phone so you can keep adding to your list. After doing this for a month, look back on all the things you wrote to give yourself a little positivity boost.

To add variety to your gratitude practice, you can also collect gratitude images. There are tons of images and image-collecting apps online. Use one of these online tools to collect images of people, places, or things that you're grateful for. These can be photos that you took, drawings you made, or images you found online. Every week, add new images to your collection. That way, you'll get a gratitude boost from seeing all the other images you collected in the past and also continue to grow your gratitude as you add new images.

Savor While You're Surfing

Too often we let the good moments we experience online pass by without truly savoring or celebrating them. When we savor these moments, we pause and attempt to fully experience the positive emotions that have arisen in that moment, and as a result, we create longer-lasting positive emotions (Quoidbach et al. 2010).

When we're surfing online or on social media, one easy way to practice savoring is by reflecting on and bringing up positive memories from the past. These days, there are usually large collections of old photos—taken by us or others we know—that can help us recall our past positive experiences.

To savor the past, look through these old photos until you find one that reminds you of a positive event that you long forgot. Spend a few moments thinking deeply about this event. As you are thinking back on the pleasant event, think about the people, smells, sounds, physical sensations, and sights that you experienced. Think about—and try to re-create—the positive emotions that you felt around the time of the event. As you are savoring, let your thoughts wander to anything else about the happy experience that makes you feel good. Then, just mentally hold on to these emotions, trying to make them as strong as possible.

We can also practice savoring elsewhere online. There are near infinite positive things we encounter that just pass us by. But if we stop for a moment to savor and appreciate these things, we can make our positive emotions last longer. So as you are surfing the Internet, pay attention anytime you experience something positive. Maybe your friend shares a story that inspires you. Maybe a colleague posts a joke that makes you laugh. Or maybe you watch cat videos or awe-inducing landscapes that make you feel happy or relaxed.

Whenever you notice yourself feeling good, pause for just a moment and pay attention to how these positive emotions feel in your body. Mentally try to hold on to these emotions by thinking about how good they feel and how much you appreciate feeling this way. As you continue to go about your day, online or offline, try to pause for a moment to savor the good feelings.

Extend Positive Moments by Sharing Them

To extend a positive moment even longer, show it, tell it, or share it with others right away. Keep in mind that the positive moment doesn't have to be big. You could simply have woken up on the right side of the bed and think, *Hey, I'm feeling great today.*

Start by sending a personal message to someone. You might call or text a friend or talk to the people around you about what you're feeling. Just be sure that you're sharing your *emotions* and not bragging.

For example, you could send the message: *Hey, I'm feeling great today. I'd love to get together with you for coffee and make my day even better.* If you don't have the time to connect with others in person, don't let it stop you from sharing your positive feelings. For example, you might say, *I'm so pumped after our meeting this afternoon. It was great seeing you.* Or you might say, *Are you watching the Olympics? That last athlete was amazing!* Or perhaps, *I was so glad to see so many people getting out to vote in last night's election.* Rather than talking about what happened to you, share your positive emotions with someone whom you want to connect with.

Use Your Imagination to Create Positive Emotions

If you're still struggling to find things to savor or be grateful for, try *imagining* situations that would make you feel positive emotions. It turns out that when we imagine things, our brains react as though these situations actually happened.

You probably already know that when you think about something bad happening, you start to feel all sorts of negative emotions as if that bad thing already happened. Just the thought of your romantic partner leaving you or losing your job might lead to intense anxiety, anger, or sadness. Our brains act as if those thoughts are real. So thinking about negative scenarios that haven't even happened is horrible for our happiness.

But on the bright side, our brains do the exact same thing if we imagine positive scenarios. By imagining all the positive things that *could* happen in our future, we can create all the positive emotions that would arise in those situations. You don't even have to imagine things that are *likely* to happen. The goal is to just imagine the things that would make you feel good. For example, maybe you imagine your boss finally praising you for something you did well, maybe you imagine spending all afternoon at an amusement park with your family, or maybe you imagine flying around town on a purple dragon. Don't limit yourself to reality. Regardless of whether or not your fantasy can come true, imagining good things makes you feel good. Almost magically, you create positive emotions out of thin air.

To try out this imagination strategy, spend a few minutes in the morning imagining the best possible day you could have while you're brushing your teeth or taking a shower. Ask yourself:

- What would happen?
- Who would you interact with?
- How would you feel?

For example, you might imagine that your morning is really productive and you get everything done that you wanted to—perhaps you'd feel a sense of accomplishment. Then, you might imagine a friend takes you out for lunch—perhaps you'd feel joyous and delighted. Then you might imagine your day ends with an easy commute and extra time to yourself—and perhaps you'd feel calm and relaxed. As you are imagining, really try to generate the emotions that would occur if your day went exactly as you imagine.

To create an imagination practice, put your phone away before you go to bed and spend a moment with your thoughts. Imagine what tomorrow could be like—not what you *think* it will be like, but what it *could* be at its best. Get creative by imagining that tomorrow you get promoted to your dream job or your office is suddenly overrun with adorable puppies. Besides putting a smile on your face, regularly using this strategy can also help you strengthen your positivity by keeping your mind more focused on positive outcomes. It gets easier to dream, which is a good thing.

As you are playing with imagination, keep in mind that imagining something won't necessarily make it come true, as some popular self-help books might suggest. Rather, using this trick can make the boring more exciting, the annoying more tolerable, and the icky more enjoyable. And when you use the positivity skills you've learned in this section, you'll be better equipped to start dealing with the hard stuff and building your resilience.

BUILD RESILIENCE

Resilience is that amazing skill that helps you recover quickly from difficulties. And as we discussed earlier in this book, the technology age is filled with new difficulties. Whether it be in response to the automation of our jobs, the hate that is spewed on social media, or pervasive media that pummels our self-esteem, resilience is a skill that is greatly needed in the technology age. When you build resilience, you'll be better able to cope with these challenges. So how do you build resilience in the technology age?

Search for Silver Linings

A few years ago, my car's transmission blew completely. If I had wanted to, I could have focused on the negative things about this experience—it cost more than a $1,000 to fix, it was one of a string of repairs on that car, and I desperately needed that car to get to work. But because I had already trained my brain to find silver linings, instead of focusing on these negatives, I actually felt grateful! I was grateful that this didn't happen on the dangerous two-hour commute

I did each day to get to and from work. I was relieved that my partner was in the car with me and he could help me get it to an auto shop that day. I even felt happy because third gear was still working, so I could drive it to the auto shop without having to pay to get it towed. When you can see the silver linings, challenges aren't as challenging.

So how do you find these mysterious silver linings? Well, you just have to make a habit of looking for them. For example, you might find that the silver lining of working a really difficult job is that you learn new skills and build character. And you might find that the silver lining of working a really easy job is that you feel relaxed and have more time to devote to other things you enjoy. Of course, this does not mean that all experiences are equally good. A crappy job is still a crappy job. All I'm saying is that we can buffer ourselves from stress and protect our happiness by recognizing that there is *some* good, even in objectively horrible situations. When you start to see the world in this way, nothing appears to be all black or all white—it's all gray.

To practice finding silver linings, first think about a slightly negative situation you experienced recently. Try not to choose an experience that is extremely negative—it's important to choose an experience that's not too bad when you are first learning how to use this technique. You can work up to harder experiences as you become more skilled. For example, maybe you forgot your lunch or you had a disagreement with a friend. Choose something small like this and write it down in your notebook.

Next, spend a few minutes trying to find silver linings. You could try to think of the benefits, think about how the situation could be worse, or brainstorm opportunities that could result from this situation in the long term. Try to search for as many silver linings as you can think of and write them down.

Ask yourself these questions to brainstorm:

- Were there, or will there be, any positive outcomes that result from this situation?

- Are you grateful for any part of this situation?

- In what ways are you better off than when you started?

- What did you learn?

- How did you grow and develop as a result of this situation?

My response regarding getting in a disagreement with a friend might look like this:

> I got in a fight with Sherry. Even though it is tough, the silver linings are (1) I stood up for myself and what I believe in, (2) it'll give us an opportunity to improve the way we communicate with each other, and (3) now I know what makes Sherry mad, so I can be more careful how I approach her in the future.

Once you have your silver linings, consider sharing your challenging situation and at least one benefit on social media with #SilverLinings. Highlighting silver linings when you share something negative online can help train your brain to do this IRL. When others see your #SilverLinings post, it may even help them try it too. You could even post a message asking your friends or family to share some of *their* #SilverLinings. For example, you could create a post asking people, *What was something crappy that happened to you, and what were the unexpected positive outcomes that resulted from it?*

By asking other people about their silver linings, I discovered that a former boss of mine once published an error in a paper, which resulted in her becoming more organized. Another person I know went through a challenging divorce and then met the love of his life. Seeing how others have found silver linings can help us learn tricks we can use in our own lives.

Maybe you've read my examples of silver linings, and they just don't jive with your experience. That's understandable, and it happens a lot because one of the most annoying phrases we can hear is, "Hey, just look at the bright side." When someone else says this, it usually backfires. So keep in mind that this technique only works if you're willing to do it and do it often. The more you practice this skill, the easier it'll become. And eventually, you won't even have to think about it anymore. You'll be like I was when my transmission blew—somehow feeling good in spite of the bad.

Find Silver Linings While Streaming Movies

If you're still having a hard time finding the silver linings in your own life, it might be easier to first practice this strategy with other people's lives. To try this, plan to practice finding silver linings next time you stream a movie or show (Troy et al. 2010). Before watching a sad or emotional movie or scene, read these instructions:

> While watching the scene or movie, think about what could be learned from the experience or imagine possible positive outcomes. With these suggestions in mind, think about what advice you would give the characters for how to feel better. When the movie is over, ask yourself, "How could you apply this advice to your own life?"

Afterward, write your response down in your notebook. See if thinking about other people's situations made it easier for you to find silver linings.

Look at Your Situation from an Outsider's Perspective

Another way to build resilience is to look at your situation as if you were "a fly on the wall" or as if you were someone else who is witnessing your situation from afar. These days, we are so immersed in our experiences—what we feel, what we think, even what we had for dinner. We think about the world from our point of view only, and we share this point of view on social media, on forums, and in comments all over the Internet. But it turns out that emotionally distancing yourself from your experience and looking at it from an outsider's perspective helps you from getting stuck in your negative emotions. As a result, you don't feel quite as bad, even when you do feel bad (Ayduk and Kross 2010).

To practice this strategy, first recall a recent stressful situation. Be sure to choose something very specific. For example, if you got in a fight with a friend about forgetting your birthday, try not to think about fights in general. Once you've chosen the situation you will use for this activity, write it down in your notebook.

Now, reimagine the stressful event from an outside observer's point of view. For example, imagine the situation from the point of view of a stranger on the street or a fly on the wall.

Ask yourself these questions and write down your responses in your notebook:

- Would the observer be able to understand why you are upset?

- Would the observer be able to see the other person's point of view?

- How would the observer evaluate the situation?

- Might this observer be more objective about the situation?

By mentally removing ourselves from our situation, we can start to get a broader perspective, which helps us bounce back more quickly and be more resilient. And guess what? You don't have to practice this skill just by writing in your notebook. You can also practice shifting your perspective by viewing other people's experiences on social media.

Next time you're on social media, pause when you come upon a friend's personal story, perhaps a story about their kids, their day, or some success that they've had. Imagine, for a moment, that you are them. Ask yourself how you would feel differently if you were in their shoes.

Now switch back to viewing their situation from your point of view. The more we practice switching between perspectives, the more we can use this skill to reduce negative emotions. As a result, we can be more resilient.

Look at Your Situation from a Different Point in Time

In addition to shifting to another *person's* perspective, we can shift to another time perspective by looking at our situation from another point in *time* (Bruehlman-Senecal and Ayduk 2015). This technique also helps dampen our emotions because we see that our negative emotions are not permanent, so we feel less afraid of them. And when we are less afraid of our emotions, we don't need to turn to our phones to distract ourselves from them.

Take a moment now to think of a negative situation in your life right now. Shift your perspective by looking at this negative situation from one year in the future: How would *you in the future* view this situation differently?

Ask yourself these questions and write down your responses in your notebook:

- In one year, how will you feel about this particular situation?

- How will this current situation affect what you're doing in one year?

- How will this current situation affect how you feel in one year?

If you'd like to make this practice work even better, show yourself just how much your emotions actually do change in a year. Use an online calendar to find the date that is one year after today. In the description box, write down how you feel right now about something that's bothering you. I'll do it right now with you. My entry looks like this:

> I'm feeling frustrated and tired because I have a health issue that is just not going away. I'm taking all sorts of meds and eating super healthy, but I'm not getting better. I can't wait to look back at this in a year when I feel better.

Set a notification in your calendar so one year from today you'll be reminded to look back on how you felt about this situation. You'll see then just how much your emotions change. We really do move on from challenges, even challenges that seem incredibly hard at the time.

Face What Makes You Feel Uncomfortable

In life, a great many things make us feel uncomfortable. Oftentimes, these are things that lead us to pick up our phone. For example, if you're worried about your finances, you may continue to shop online and avoid looking at your credit card balance. Or if you have a bad day at work, you may want to go home and binge-watch movies just to forget about it all. These actions seem innocent enough, but usually they function as emotional avoidance. Avoiding our emotions can be dangerous because the emotions fester, build up, and never get resolved (Chapman, Gratz, and Brown 2006). When we turn to our phone or other technology instead of dealing with our negative emotions, they stay with us. We carry these buried emotions with us wherever we go, and they can pop out at inopportune moments and in really weird ways. These emotions can even morph into health issues, relationship issues, or work issues. And this makes it even harder to be resilient because we are not only dealing with our current challenges but also the remnants of the challenges we avoided dealing with in the past.

Until my midtwenties, I did everything I could to avoid feeling negative emotions. But these suppressed emotions just kept popping up in the weirdest situations, like some perverse whack-a-mole game. One day on the way to work, I got pulled over for speeding, and it sent me into a full-on sobbing panic attack. It was super embarrassing and completely inappropriate, but it was an aha moment for me. Instead of going to work that day, I drove straight to the medical center. While still in the midst of panic and gasping for air, I asked to see a therapist.

Over the next few months, this therapist taught me a lot about how to stop avoiding my negative emotions and just experience my discomfort (Hayes, Strosahl, and Wilson 2012). How did she do it? She told me to "run at the dog." What she meant was that instead of running away from our fears, we should run right at them. Don't inch toward them; don't walk toward them. Run! This one piece of advice has probably done more for me than any other piece of advice I've gotten because it gave me more control of my emotions. I no longer feel like I need a drink to relax, need to hide who I am to keep the peace, or need to use my smartphone to avoid feeling awkward. Emotions just don't seem quite as scary.

Take a moment now to think about the ways you avoid facing your emotions. Ask yourself these questions and write down your answers in your notebook.

- What emotions are least comfortable for you? Anger? Anxiety? Sadness? Embarrassment?

- What actions do you engage in to avoid these emotions? Do you pull out your phone? Go on social media? Watch videos? Something else?

- Instead of avoiding emotions, what actions could you take to "run at the dog"?

If you are trying to outsmart your smartphone, your response might look like this:

I hate feeling embarrassment. To avoid this feeling, I take selfies dozens of times so they look perfect. To run at the dog, I'm going to take a photo of myself first thing in the morning before I've cleaned myself up and post it on social media.

Does running at the dog seem terrifying? It's supposed to. That's the point. If it doesn't, then you haven't yet found what *really* scares you. Keep looking. And when you have found the emotions and experiences that you're avoiding, stare them down and take them on with gusto. I won't lie; it's hard at first. But pretty soon, you'll be better able to cope with even the things that used to scare you most. You'll be more resilient. And you won't need your phone to distract you from your emotions.

Use Your Negative Emotions to Propel You Forward

I've spent a lot of time in this chapter helping you learn how to increase positive emotions and decrease negative emotions. Before we move on, it's important for you to know that negative emotions are completely normal, healthy (Davis et al. 2014), and even beneficial at times (Keltner and Gross 1999). For example, negative emotions like sadness and grief help communicate to others that we need their support and kindness. Negative emotions like anger help motivate us to take action, make changes in our lives, and maybe even change the world. And negative emotions like anxiety and stress, in small doses, help us be more productive and efficient. At their heart, all emotions have important purposes.

You already know that avoiding your negative emotions can be harmful. But you have to be careful when managing negative emotions too. Decreasing your negative emotions with healthy strategies can still leave you feeling stuck and unable to get your needs met if you still don't understand where these emotions came from in the first place.

So when life throws you into a ditch and you feel crappy, ask yourself the following questions and write the answers down in your notebook.

- Are these negative emotions trying to teach me something?

- Would decreasing these negative emotions (with strategies like finding silver linings) fail to address the root causes of these emotions?

- Would it be better to keep the emotions and use them to fuel actions—actions like getting out of your crappy job, asking for help to cope with a loss, or starting a movement to address some social injustice?

Your negative emotions are trying to tell you something. So before stopping them, pause and reflect on whether you can use these emotions to fuel some positive change in your life or in the world. By taking these short pauses, you'll be less likely to prioritize increasing your current happiness at the expense of your long-term happiness.

FINAL THOUGHTS

Managing your emotions well can truly change your life, helping you finally tolerate challenges, outsmart your smartphone, and develop long-lasting happiness. Hopefully the tips in this chapter helped you start building these skills. Keep it up, and you'll see more improvement in time.

Practice Kindness

Technology continues to get more advanced. It is now at the point where algorithms decide what we see. Our social media pages link us to people who are similar to us. We only see the content that we will be most likely to click on. And we only read news that confirms the beliefs we already have. As a result, we all now exist in our own bubbles—we only socialize with people who are like us, we only understand the struggles of people like us, and we only hear the opinions of people who agree with us.

You may be wondering, *What's so bad about that?* Algorithms show us what we want to see, and that makes us happy, right? Well, sort of. You may be happier in that moment, just as you might be happier after eating a big, unhealthy piece of cake or drinking a six-pack of beer. But just like these other enjoyable but unhealthy behaviors, consumption of our favorite online content can hurt us in the long run.

The longer we stay in our bubbles, the more we think that people different from us are wrong, bad, or simply crazy because we don't know or understand these people. First, this prevents us from making new connections, which you already learned in step three is key to your happiness. But it's even worse than that. Our lack of empathy and insight into others often leads us to be unkind to them—online, in-person, or even just in our thoughts. This is a big problem because it turns out that kindness is like rocket fuel for our happiness—the kinder we are, the happier we become. And the more people we can extend that kindness to, the greater potential we have to create enduring happiness.

Now don't worry. I'm not asking you to be super polite or kind or Pollyannaish all the time—that would be exhausting. In fact, these types of kindnesses can feel forced or annoying. Like when we are just nice to someone because we're supposed to or we help someone out because we feel like we should. Practicing kindness in ways that don't feel right can leave us feeling depleted instead of rejuvenated. So if you want to experience the real (and huge!) benefits of kindness, you have to learn how to practice kindness in ways that work *for you*.

In this chapter, you'll search inside yourself to learn how to practice kindness in the ways that fit you. You'll do this by identifying your values, finding your purpose, and choosing ways to make positive impacts that matter to you. As a result of this exploration, you'll discover the type of kindness that actually feels good to you, the type of kindness that you'll *want* to share with everyone, the type of kindness that'll boost your happiness in both the short term and longer term.

In this chapter, you'll learn how to:

- live your values

- find your purpose

- make positive impacts.

LIVE YOUR VALUES

We so often go through life without paying much attention. We're distracted—by work, by family responsibilities, and now by our phones too. As a result, we move from one thing to the next without pausing to consider whether our actions reflect our values. Now, it's okay that our actions do not always reflect our *ideal self*—that perfect self that we wish we were. No one is perfect, and it is not healthy to create a long list of things we "should" be doing. But when we go through life without following our value compass, we can lose ourselves, our natural modes of kindness, and our ability to generate real happiness.

One friend of mine from high school—a strong, supportive, selfless person—was always the one to give to others. Forgot your lunch?

No worries, she'd take you out. Pursuing a new side hustle? She'd be your first customer. She delighted in the ability to be able to help others with the resources she had.

After high school, we lost touch. Then one day she reached out asking me for something she needed. I happily obliged and gave her what she asked for. But I soon learned that she had sold everything she had for drugs and was asking friends and family for things to sell for drugs. Never had she been willing to take advantage of others. But when in the throes of her addiction, she lost track of who she was and what mattered to her.

Thankfully, she recovered from her addiction. But she *didn't* recover her values right away. It wasn't until later, when she had kids, that she started living her values again. I think her kids helped remind her what mattered to her. She now takes great pleasure in supporting them, helping them grow, and helping them experience all life has to offer. She's found a new way to live her values that fit her new life.

Because I was looking in from the outside, it was easier to see my friend's values and how they affected her happiness. But values are not always so easy to see when we're looking at ourselves. Because each of us holds very different values, it can look very different when we lose sight of them. This is why it's so important to identify our values and clarify for ourselves what actions we need to take to live our values.

If we take the time to really understand our values, we'll see that they not only help us feel happier—because we are now living a life that feels right to us—our values also compel us to act in ways that are kinder. They help us pursue our purpose and make positive impacts in other people's lives. This is why living our values helps us create an upward spiral of happiness.

Identify Your Values

By identifying our values, we can begin to design a life that feels good to us. Remember, everyone holds different values, and you are the only one who gets to decide what your values are—not your parents, not your partner, not your boss.

You may already have a sense of what your main values are. But it's helpful to identify them all. You could be living some and not others, and you may benefit from focusing on some values more than others.

To get started, peruse the values list below. In your notebook, write down any of the values that you hold. If you think of values you hold that are not on this list, please do add them. This list is far from comprehensive, and there may be something really important to you that is not listed.

Values List

Authenticity	Adventure	Balance
Bravery	Compassion	Challenge
Citizenship	Community	Creativity
Curiosity	Determination	Fairness
Freedom	Friendships	Fun
Generosity	Growth	Honesty
Influence	Justice	Kindness
Knowledge	Leadership	Learning
Love	Loyalty	Openness
Optimism	Recognition	Respect
Responsibility	Security	Self-Respect
Social Connection	Spirituality	Stability
Status	Wealth	Wisdom

Once you have your list in your notebook, circle (or underline if you're using a digital notebook) your "top" most important three values. For each of these top values, write down at least three actions that you could take to live these values. If you value loyalty, for example, actions might include forgiving a friend for a betrayal, negotiating fair treatment at work to ensure you can remain loyal, or choosing not to engage in extra-marital affairs.

If you are trying to outsmart your smartphone, for example, your response might look like this:

Loyalty:

1) Call my parents to let them know I still care about them.

2) Apologize to Jane for bailing on her all those times to play online poker.

3) Schedule a monthly get together with my friends to rebuild fractured relationships.

Remember, each of us is dealing with different life challenges, so the actions we need to take to live our values will be very different.

Next, write down one thing you have done that goes against each your top three values. If you value optimism, for example, worrying about the future is likely an example of how you're not living your values.

If you are trying to outsmart your smartphone, your response might look like this:

Optimism: I worry that if I leave my phone at home, I'll miss out an inside joke with friends or fall behind on my email.

Lastly, write down one thing you could do differently next time to better live each value. For optimism, maybe instead of worrying about the future, you could think about what might go right, what you might learn, or what cool things you have to look forward to in the future.

If you are trying to outsmart your smartphone, your response might look like this:

Optimism: I look forward to being more present during my interactions with friends because I won't have my phone with me to distract me.

As you are doing this activity, you may discover that there are easy ways that you could live in closer alignment with you values. However, some of the actions you identified may be harder to follow through with. Maybe you would need to leave your phone at home. Maybe you would need to stop drinking. Maybe you would need to have some difficult conversations. It's quite easy to go with the flow and lose sight of our values; it's a lot harder to do what's right for us and our long-term happiness. But because you've been building key happiness skills as you've been reading this book, I think you're ready for what comes next—living your values.

Identify What Leads You Away from Your Values

When I first did this activity, I discovered that respect is one of my top values. I was living this value in some ways, with some people, and in some situations, but I had some major gaps. For example, I could be really mean to my partner, criticizing him for the smallest things and judging him for his actions and decisions.

One day, as I walked to work, vacant, feeling like a shell of my former self, I started wondering why I felt so hollow. I'm not sure how or why, but I had an epiphany. I wasn't living my value of respect. I so deeply wanted to be treated with respect, yet I was failing to respect the person closest to me. I had identified an important value that I wasn't living fully. Now, I just needed to figure out why.

To start exploring what leads you away from your values, take a look at the values list you created earlier in this section. For each of your top three most important values, ask yourself these questions and record your answers in your notebook:

- Are there any people whom you have a difficult time living this value with? For example, maybe it's your romantic partner, parent, sibling, coworker, or friend.

- Where are you and what are you doing when you fail to live your values? For example, maybe you're at work, at home, out at the bar, on social media, in the car, or at the day-care center.

- Is there anything else that makes it difficult for you to live your values? For example, maybe you live your values in the morning but not at night, when in your hometown but not on vacation, or on Monday but not Friday.

My response regarding the value of respect might look like this:

I have a difficult time living my value of respect with my partner. I am especially rude and disrespectful if we've been drinking, regardless of the time of day or location.

Once you've identified the external events that lead you away from your values, it's important that you explore why these experiences affect you this way. Ask yourself what thoughts, feelings, or bodily sensations lead you to act differently than you would like to. Write your answers down in your notebook.

My response regarding my value of respect might look like this:

It's hard for me to live this value when I'm not feeling respected or appreciated. I start to get agitated, and then I lash out.

By identifying the emotions, thoughts, or associated bodily sensations that lead us to act in opposition to our values, we can start to better understand why we act the way we do.

Overcome Value Conflicts

It is usually the case that our actions—even actions that go against our values—serve some kind of emotional function. In other words, these actions make us feel better, at least temporarily. This presents a conflict between our value and our emotions.

The truth is that is if you're having a hard time living your values, you likely have at least one value conflict. How do you know if you have a conflict? Well, if acting in opposition to your values satisfies some unmet emotional need, you have a conflict. You either live your value or meet your need. This can feel like an impossible choice.

When I first explored my value of respect, the idea of changing my behavior and living my value made my stomach sink. I felt disrespected and unappreciated by my partner, so the last thing I wanted to do was be respectful to him. It felt like I had to choose between being respectful and being respected, a lose-lose situation. Indeed, I had run right into a value conflict.

Because we humans prioritize feeling good in the short term, emotional needs almost always trump our values. For example, maybe your boss was hit as a child, leading him to both value freedom yet have a strong need for power. So despite valuing freedom, he micromanages his employees to gain the sense of power he so desperately needs. Or maybe your neighbor was criticized for her appearance growing up, leading her to value acceptance yet have a strong need to feel good about her appearance. So despite valuing acceptance, she makes fun of how people look to make herself feel better.

It seems there are an infinite number of value conflicts that could arise. By identifying our value conflicts, our actions—even actions were not proud of—start to make a lot more sense to us. You're not a bad person; your brain is just making a mental calculation and choosing what it believes will make you happiest in the moment. Unfortunately, your brain's calculation usually shortchanges both your values and your needs. So how do you shift this tendency? Learn how to get your needs met in new ways—ways that don't conflict with your values.

To start, you need to identify any value conflicts you may have. Take a moment now to reflect on what you get from going against your values. Ask yourself the following questions and write your answers down in your notebook.

- What's the upside of not living your value?

- What positive emotions are you feeling? Excited? Safe? Loved?

- What needs are being satisfied by not living your value?

My response regarding the value of respect might look like this:

> When I am disrespectful to my partner, I feel empowered. I feel better about myself (in the short term) because I have put him down.

As you can see from my example, not living my value helped me meet my needs but in an unhealthy way. Most of us struggle to meet our needs in healthy ways, but we must change this if we want to overcome the value conflicts that shortchange our happiness.

So, ask yourself: "How else you could get your needs met? How could you generate the positive emotions you desire without abandoning your values?" For example, the man who feels powerless could create and lead an online group on a topic he cares about, helping him gain a sense of power with a more positive outcome. You can do things like this too. So take a moment now to write in your notebook the healthy things you can do to start getting your needs met.

My response regarding the value of respect might look like this:

> I need to calmly but honestly communicate my feelings to my partner and help him understand what makes me feel disrespected. Then I need to make it clear that if he's not willing to make an effort to help me get my needs met, I can no longer be in the marriage.

As this example demonstrates, living your values requires a level of self-awareness, honesty, and bravery that can be difficult to achieve. So give it time and be patient with yourself. Take one small action at a time and try to go easy on yourself. If you don't yet feel ready for this, spend more time building the skills in the earlier steps of this book. The skills you learn in the earlier steps can help you accomplish these later steps more easily.

FIND YOUR PURPOSE

When you are living your values, all the experiences you have and all the actions you take will feel like a better fit, so you are more likely to stumble upon your life purpose (or multiple life purposes!) along the way. And because your life purpose is really just a collection of value-driven actions that lead you toward a particular goal, the activities in the last section can better prepare you for this set of activities on finding your purpose. So let's take advantage of this moment and use it to help you find your purpose.

Find Your Big Goals by Exploring Your Pain

About a decade ago, a friend of mine fell twenty feet from a water tower, hitting his head on both a steel beam and the concrete below. He was immediately rushed to the hospital. Luckily, he survived, but he was in a coma and sustained a devastating brain injury—over 90 percent of patients with this brain injury never regain consciousness, and most of those who do will remain in a persistent vegetative state. Like them, when my friend woke from his coma, he didn't eat, walk, or talk for months.

But there is a silver lining to this story. At a pivotal moment during his recovery, my friend discovered the role of nutrition in brain health. He studied this subject like his life depended on it...because it did. Overcoming his brain injury with nutrition became his life purpose. And miraculously, he healed himself. Today, he is more devoted to his purpose than anyone I've ever met. He built a business around his purpose and helps people all over the country overcome their brain injuries.

This is an incredible story, but it is also filled with incredible pain. And I often see this among the people who have a strong purpose. That's because powerful pain often leads to powerful purpose. Of course, we all have experienced pain—pain that made us see something differently or value something that others don't. Hiding in our pain are the clues to our purpose. We just have to look for them.

So take a moment now to ask yourself: "Did you experience any pain that affected your goals in life? Is there a challenge that you feel compelled to help others overcome?" Take a moment now to write your answers in your notebook. Write down everything you think of as your insights can provide clues that can help you uncover your purpose.

My friend's response might look like this:

> I sustained a major brain injury that changed everything in my life. I had to work very hard to find the information that saved me, and now it is my goal to make it easier for others to get this information to overcome their brain injuries.

Purpose isn't immediately obvious for most of us, so don't get down on yourself if you don't have a story like this that makes your purpose crystal clear. Give it time and keep exploring.

Explore Possible Paths to Your Purpose

In graduate school, one of my classmates decided she wanted to be a therapist. She already knew her purpose was to advance the field of psychology, and she was already conducting important academic research. But she wanted to help people, and she figured therapy was a good way to use her skill set. So she joined a training program to become a therapist.

After her first week, she started to get really nervous. She worked hard to prepare for each client but found herself dreading it. After a month, she was exhausted. The stress of advising people wore her down and tore her away from her other activities. She started having serious doubts about whether she could continue. *Is this for me? Can I handle it? Maybe I should just give up and try something else,* she pondered. After the training was over, she knew for sure that it was not the right way to pursue her purpose. But the experience was not wasted. She now knew *for sure* that pursuing a career as a therapist was not a fit for her, something she'd wondered about for years. She could move forward with graduate school with renewed vigor. And she did. She ended up being one of the most successful researchers in my class.

This experience of trying something and realizing it's not right happens to us all. It doesn't mean we're failures. It means we are brave because we were willing to try. Most of us don't find our purpose on the first try, so we just have to get back up and keep trying new things. Fortunately, our bodies give us clues as to which actions are a good fit for our purpose and which actions are not. For example, if we use our mindfulness skills to pay attention to our energy level, enthusiasm, and determination, we can figure out if we're on the right track.

When we know which tasks give us joy, we can better find the right path toward our purpose. So take a moment now to reflect on how different tasks make you feel. Ask yourself: "Which activities make you feel energized, enthusiastic, or determined?" For example, maybe you feel energized when working with others but not when working alone. Maybe you feel enthusiastic when you're reading, talking, building something with your hands, organizing, or solving problems. Or maybe you feel determined to finish every book you pick up, but you never finish a meal. Basically, try to figure out what day-to-day tasks you love to do so much that you lose track of time, maybe even forgetting to eat or go to the bathroom. Take a moment now to write your answers in your notebook.

My friend who sustained the brain injury might have a response that looks like this:

> I am energized by talking to people, exchanging ideas, and sharing what I've learned with others.

Lastly, use your responses to figure out one possible purpose. This purpose should include doing a task that energizes you (from this activity) to achieve a goal that matters to you (from the last activity). In your notebook, write down as least one possible purpose.

My friend who sustained the brain injury might have a response that looks like this:

Maybe I could create a podcast to talk with experts on brain injury and share my insights. Or I could try coaching others who need my help. I'll try these tasks first to see if they are a good fit for me.

Now that you have possible purposes, schedule one hour sometime in the next week that you'll spend trying a purpose out. See how it feels to you. When you are done, reflect on how it made you feel to see if you want to continue or experiment with another purpose.

Avoid Purpose Traps

We've all been told we should pursue this or that career, spend our time building specific skills, or use our spare time in specific ways. Whether it's our parents, friends, mentors, or media, most of us go through life with lots of people telling us what we *should* do. There is nothing wrong with listening to their suggestions—the problem only comes when ignore what is right for us.

Warning! This is a big trap that keeps so many people from living their purpose. I hear the same story a lot—so-and-so pursued a corporate job because that what's they were told to do, told by their parents, their partners, or by society. Now they've realized this isn't their purpose, and they're not sure how to find a new path.

If this sounds like you, try taking a deep dive into what's working and what's not.

Ask yourself: "What parts of your life are working, and what parts aren't?" Take a moment now to write your answers down in your notebook.

A response might look like this:

I like my day-to-day tasks—working with teams, helping coworkers, and coaching others—but my job doesn't really fit my values or goals. I'd really like to apply my skills toward helping the environment.

Try to figure out what you need to change and what can stay the same. This way, you can make smaller changes that won't be as scary. And don't give up. It's a process, and it takes time, exploration, and reflection to find the path that will create the most meaningful life, *for you.*

MAKE POSITIVE IMPACTS

Although living our values and pursuing our purpose might seem like self-focused acts, they are actually quite good at helping us practice more kindness. Why? Because living our values involves cultivating those values, not just in ourselves but in others. We can't live our value of freedom if we are trapping others. We can't live our value of fairness if we always take a bigger piece of the pie. And we can't live our value of wealth if we make it impossible for others to become wealthy. Values are inherently social. So living them incidentally results in positive impacts on the lives of others.

For example, imagine you value adventure. To live your value, you decide to stop binge-watching videos online and instead start organizing wild adventures. Sometimes you invite your friends and family. You've just made it easier for these people to *also* experience more adventure. Or, imagine you value leadership. You decide to stop criticizing others and instead try to be a better mentor. As a result, everyone you lead benefits more from your leadership. Or, imagine you value stability. You start saving extra money for a rainy day. When the car breaks down or your family has an unexpected health bill, you can afford it. Suddenly, you've saved your family from extra stress as well.

It's amazing how every value-driven action has a positive *reaction* in the world around you. Human beings were designed to support each other, and when we do, we are rewarded for it. Pursuing happiness only seems to fail when we do it selfishly and in isolation.

You'll see similar results when pursuing your purpose. If you do it in isolation, it doesn't feel quite complete. For example, maybe you're an artist and you spend every day joyfully painting. But sharing your work with others, enabling them to enjoy it too is likely to be what really makes you feel a greater sense of purpose. Or maybe you're a chef. You could cook nonstop, but if no one is there to eat your food, do you still feel a sense of purpose? Or maybe you make widgets in the widget factory. It's knowing that people benefit from these widgets that makes your work feel meaningful. Pursuing our purpose, just like living our values, is an act of kindness that positively impacts others. But even better, these are the types of kindness that feel really good because they fit *our* needs too.

Technology sometimes leads us to pursue happiness in nonsocial ways, which don't have nearly the benefits of pursuing happiness in social ways. But on the bright side, technology *has* created many new opportunities for us to live our values, pursue our purpose, and make positive impacts in people's lives. By learning how to take advantage of these opportunities, you can use start using technology in ways that generate more kindness and therefore, more happiness.

Use the Internet to Do Good in the World

You are probably familiar with traditional volunteer jobs—volunteering at a homeless shelter, taking donations to Goodwill, or phonebanking for a political candidate. More power to you if decide to volunteer your time to local organizations in order to make a positive impact. But in the technology age, there are all sorts of additional ways to make positive impacts online. You could do good for your town, your country, or even the globe, all from your smartphone or computer. It's up to you to figure out how to live your values and purpose, making a positive impact in the ways that work *for you*. But here are some ideas.

Join a Mission-Oriented Online Group or Organization

One way to make a positive impact (and as a bonus, build positive relationships with others) is by joining a mission-oriented online group. There are now tons of online groups that focus on achieving specific goals—for example, electing a particular political candidate, addressing an important social problem, or fundraising for an important cause. Joining one of these mission-oriented groups can be a great way to dip your toes into making positive impacts with very little time investment or risk. You can volunteer your time, donate money to the cause, or both.

When I first started helping mission-oriented groups, it was brand new to me. I was not really the type to volunteer or donate. So I started slowly. I donated a small amount to a political campaign, donated to support a blogger whose writing I enjoy, and tried volunteering at one organization whose mission I believed in. What happened? I fell in love with how it made me feel. Although my free time is limited, I started volunteering a few hours per week and seeking out other ways to make positive impacts. I swear, this activity made me happier than perhaps any other strategy in this book. It has multiplied my happiness because it doesn't just feel good in the moment—the positive feelings of having done something good for the world stay with you all day, and sometimes for several days.

If you're like me and this is new to you, just try a few different things until you find something that makes you feel good. Use your notebook to reflect on how each experience went—pay special attention to how each experience makes you feel in the moment and later that day or week. If your first attempt is not quite the right fit, try out other actions to discover what boosts your happiness the most.

Start Your Own Website, Blog, or Channel

Got some skills or knowledge that could benefit others? Then you might want to make your own website, blog, or video channel. This is another way that technology can be leveraged to make positive impacts in the lives of others. And it doesn't have to be anything fancy. When I first started my website, http://www.berkeleywellbeing.com, it was just a collection of resources, tools, and tips to help people grow their well-being. I'd never built a website before, but I wanted to share the insights that I was discovering—insights that didn't seem to be available anywhere else. As a result of spending just a few hours per week on my website, I am now able to provide just a little bit of support to thousands of people. Knowing that gives me a warm, fuzzy feeling inside.

Ask yourself, "Do you have some skill, insight, or information that you think would benefit others—for example, how to fix something, how to do something technical, or how to make life easier in some way? Or might you want to share some part of yourself with the world?" For example, your writing, art, videos, ideas, or something else? If so, it might be worth sharing your gifts online—you just never know how much you might help someone else.

Engage in More Generosity

Lucky for us, it's our default to be generous. When we give to someone we care about, we make it more likely for them to give to us, making us more likely to give to them, and so forth. In fact, regions of the brain associated with pleasure, social connection, and trust light up when we're generous, making us feel all warm and gooey inside. As a bonus, if someone else sees us do something kind or generous, it makes *them* feel more optimistic and more likely to be generous too (Nook et al. 2016). Even saying a simple "thank-you" can inspire you, and those watching you, to be more generous. This is how generosity creates a ripple effect, helping us all feel happier and less lonely. So what stops us? Why aren't we all just generous all the time?

It turns out that building our positivity skills helps us get more out of generosity. For example, positive emotions—like gratitude, joy, or awe—make us more likely to give. The happier we feel when we give, the more likely we are to give to others again in the future. And the more grateful we are, in general, the more we enjoy the experience of giving.

Even if we have some work to do building our positivity skills (see step 4), we can still benefit from generosity, as long as we don't accidentally override our natural inclination to be generous by over-relying on the "thinking" parts of our brain. If we overthink kindness, we may come up with reasons for why we shouldn't give—maybe we want to buy something for ourselves or we're afraid of not having enough. But if our goal is happiness, that's a big mistake. We feel happier giving to others than when we spend money on ourselves, not to mention those gifts may make others feel happier too (Aknin, Dunn, and Norton 2012). So watch out for fear or self-focus, which can convince you that generosity is not for you.

Once we open to trying generosity as a strategy for building happiness, how might we do it? Well, we could give gifts on holidays, to acknowledge accomplishments, or just because we felt like it (that's my favorite time to give a gift). We can also practice random acts of kindness—for example, by leaving a kind note for a coworker or buying a gift for our significant other "just because."

To make giving even more rewarding, focus on giving in ways that make a positive impact in someone else's life (Aknin et al. 2013). The more we believe that what we give will be valuable or useful to others, the better it feels to us. And the more we know about how the receiver will use the gift, the more we enjoy giving. We really do want to know not only that we *are* making a difference, but also *how* we are making a difference. So give thoughtfully and intentionally (Nelson et al. 2015). It feels better—both to us and to the gift recipient.

FINAL THOUGHTS

When you live your values, pursue your purpose, and find ways to make positive impacts in people's lives, your kindness has ripple effects that grow happiness both in you and those around you. As a result, you multiply your happiness. Hopefully, this chapter gave you some good tips that'll help you implement the type of kindness that feels good to you.

Be True to Yourself

When you are building new skills, you can't just keep doing the exact same things over and over again and expect to improve. You have to challenge yourself, right? For example, if you were improving your math skills, you might start with addition, but eventually you'd have to challenge yourself to learn subtraction, multiplication, and division. Well, the same is true for happiness. Once you've built some of your skills, you'll need to push yourself to build harder skills if you want to keep growing and keep increasing your happiness.

In this chapter, we'll talk about the skills that are more challenging to build in the technology age, skills like being yourself, speaking up for yourself, and opening yourself up to others. Although these skills are not necessarily challenging for everyone (remember we all have our own strengths and weaknesses), these skills tend to be harder for many people because they require that you risk being judged, rejected, or even abandoned by others. Luckily, you're better prepared to take this step now because you've already started building the other skills in the earlier chapters of this book—skills that can help you better handle your fear of rejection, pay attention to how you really feel, and build new relationships that'll support you.

Although building these skills can be scary and even cause you pain in the short term, what emerges in the long term is a sense of true acceptance of yourself and others. Finally you can live your life, authentically, on your own terms.

In this chapter, you'll learn how to:

- be yourself

- speak up for yourself

- open yourself to others.

BE YOURSELF

Our daily lives consist of us consuming media and social media. We absorb unrealistic expectations for what we should look like, how our romantic relationships should be, and even what we should be doing between the sheets with our sexual partners. It's no wonder our social media profiles are merely presentations of who we think we should be and not reflections of who we really are (Panger 2017). We're just trying to fit in, be liked, and be accepted by other human beings, and that's completely normal. We might even think, *People wouldn't like us if we showed who we really are.*

Personal relationships are so important to us that doing anything that could threaten those relationships can feel extra scary—*We already feel lonely and disconnected. Why on earth would we want to be ourselves if that might chase people away?* Revealing our true selves can feel like a huge risk now that we live in world where everyone is presenting themselves as perfect, attractive, and happy. What if we don't feel like we are any of these things? Will being who we really are scare people away? Will everyone just suddenly abandon us?

Being yourself can feel risky, and it is. There may be people in your life who have fully bought into the idea that being a certain way and presenting a certain image is all that matters. And if you start showing your true self, these people may indeed treat you differently. But if you have to hide who you really are to be around these people, it's likely that you'll end up feeling lost, lonely, or even worthless. By being someone you are not, you are telling yourself that who you *really* are isn't okay.

When we pretend to be someone we are not, we can even harm our feelings of connection with others. If other people don't ever get to know who you really are, then you can never quite feel comfortable with others. You might not feel accepted or understood because you've not yet given others a chance to accept or understand you. For example, for many years, I would always play the music that my friends liked when we would spend time together at my house. In this small way, I was preventing them from getting to know the real me. One day, I just got tired of pretending. Instead, I blasted Britney Spears—an unpopular musician in my friend group, but one I loved nonetheless. What happened? They didn't judge me at all. In fact, they playfully teased me, and I felt *closer* to them as a result. So rather than letting fear drive our self-expression, we need to learn how to accept ourselves and truly be who we are.

Accept Yourself

Media (and social media) can make us feel unattractive. Models and actors are attractive, of course, but now even our friends on social media have Photoshopped their pictures to perfection, often making us feel unattractive by comparison (Barlett, Vowels, and Saucier 2008).

Lots of research shows the more media we consume with attractive people in it, the worse we feel about ourselves. But because media now provides us with much of our companionship, entertainment, and good memories, we don't want to give it up. We keep watching, even as media subtly tells us we're not good enough so many times that we start to believe it's true. So we have to start shifting our beliefs in ways that help us more easily accept who we are.

Identify Negative Self-Talk

One of the ways we can better accept ourselves is to identify and challenge our negative self-talk. We always have these inner monologues chirping away at us, interpreting the events happening all around us. For many of us, this self-talk is highly negative. For example, we might think, *I'm ugly*, or *My life sucks*, when we watch TV or look at social media. Or we might think, *He hates me*, if a friend posts a picture of a fun time that we weren't invited to. We could stop some of this negative self-talk by simply limiting our media and social media time, but negative self-talk can show up in other areas of our life too. So it's a good idea to work on shifting our inner dialogues to be a bit nicer toward ourselves.

Whenever you're feeling angry, anxious, or upset, pause and take a moment to reflect on your thoughts. Give it a try now. Think of some way that you put yourself down. Then, in your notebook, write out answers to these questions:

- Are my thoughts based on facts, or are they my interpretations?

- What might other explanations or interpretations be?

- How likely is it that this is as bad as I think it is?

- Are there any silver linings?

- Is there anything I can do to improve this situation?

Challenging your self-talk can help you better accept yourself and your situation so you can more easily be yourself with ease, both online and offline.

Celebrate Your Strengths

In addition to negative self-talk, we can also easily slide into the habit of focusing on our weaknesses instead of celebrating our strengths. We all suck at things. In fact, we all suck at most things, and that's okay. When we focus on these things instead of focusing on what we're good at, we can really hurt our self-esteem and get increasingly scared to be who we really are.

For example, I sometimes put myself down because I'm not great at maintaining friendships. I'm an introvert, I don't like texting, and I often feel shy about asking people to meet in person. But if we get down on ourselves regularly for the things we're not good at, it's going to be hard to like ourselves as much as we could. So, in addition to trying to improve our weaknesses, we have to remind ourselves of what we *are* good at. For example, I'm friendly, smart, and good at gardening. If we think about it, each of us has many, many strengths. Even if each these strengths are small, they add up. By identifying our strengths, we realize, hey, our weird, one-of-a-kind self is pretty awesome after all.

Give it go now. In your notebook, list ten of your strengths. Now don't worry about whether they are big strengths or small strengths. Maybe you take good care of your pet, maybe you're a good listener, maybe you always finish every book you read, or maybe you make really fantastic French toast. You rock at so many things. Don't forget them!

Once you are done listing your strengths, just pause for a moment and give yourself a pat on the back for being awesome at these things.

Express Your True Self

What else stops us from being ourselves? Mostly, it's our fear of what other people might think about us if we showed our true self. For example, maybe our friends all have the same opinion about a political topic, so we decide not to share our different point of view. Maybe our friends like a particular TV show, so we decide not talk about the shows *we* like. Or maybe our friends enjoy dining at fancy restaurants, so we decide not to invite them to our house for the cozy dinner we really prefer. We hold back because we are afraid of the possible consequences.

It's human nature for us to want to show the best sides of ourselves (Goffman 1959). And holding back our opinions occasionally is a necessary part of life. In fact, it can help make our relationships a bit easier and more enjoyable. In our in-person interactions, we have all navigated how to balance self-expression with social harmony. But now, in the technology age, we have to navigate this challenge in a whole new environment—on the Internet, through text, images, or video. We have no model to follow, so we just do what everybody else does. As a result, we show only a sliver of who we really are—the best sliver of ourselves (Panger 2017).

We don't share everything about ourselves, in part, for good reason—we don't want everyone we've ever met to know every little thing about us. But we get into trouble now in the technology age because our self-expression can easily become a show designed to evoke a response in others. The result? Few of the people in our lives know who we really are deep down. We might even start to forget who we really are deep down.

So how do we know whether our expressions have become presentations *for an audience* rather than expressions of who we really are? Well, we might start to wonder, *Who is that person we pretend to be on social media—the one with the perfect clothes, the Photoshopped body, and the biggest smile you've ever seen?* Or we might start to notice that we post pictures online, not to show to others but rather to make others *think* something specific about us. To start expressing ourselves more authentically, we'll have to use our newfound mindfulness skills to pay more attention to *why* we choose to post what we post.

As a start, take a moment now to write the answers to the following questions in your notebook.

- What is your goal when you post a video online?

- What is your goal when you post an image online?

- What is your goal when you post a message, comment, or opinion online?

- What is your goal when you share content online?

Now reflect on your answers. Do you engage in any online behavior for the primary purpose of making other people think or feel a particular way *about you?* This is the type of contrived self-expression that can lead you away from yourself.

To continue building this skill, for the next week, pay attention each time you post something online. Ask yourself, "Is this a representation of who you really are?" If not, don't post it. If it is, then let others know by adding #TrueSelf.

Show Your Vulnerability

Another important step to being ourselves is showing our vulnerability. Most of us, myself included, don't really want to show others the parts of us that we don't like—the parts that scare us or make us feel ashamed, embarrassed, or weak. It's not so easy to share these parts of ourselves. We worry, *What if others change their opinion of us, reject us, or abandon us?* It's scary to be so openly vulnerable. It can feel like opening up an old wound and telling others right where to poke us. But to fully be ourselves, we have to be *our full selves.* We can't just pick and choose the parts that we like; we can't just show the manicured, Photoshopped version of ourselves.

To be our true self, we could practice being more vulnerable on social media. I've seen some great examples of this recently. For example, some people I know recently posted about having herpes and IBS. Sharing these not-so-desirable personal details made these people vulnerable. But by being willing to be vulnerable, other people felt comfortable admitting that they deal with these common problems too. Others showed their support. And still others showed their appreciation for the honesty, something that is exceedingly rare, especially online. This is how authenticity, honesty, and vulnerability create more meaningful connections and generate more happiness.

Once we start feeling more comfortable with ourselves, we can also choose specific people or opportune moments to show our vulnerability. Whether we share our personal stories with everyone or just a few people we feel close to is up to us. For most of us, being vulnerable constantly would be too intense. Besides, we want to spend some of our time focusing on being positive, mindful, and resilient. The goal here is to be all of yourself, at least some of the time.

I'll admit, this step is not easy. I struggle a lot with being vulnerable in front of other people. I like people to think I have everything under control. I mean, I'm writing a self-help book for goodness sake.

I should have my shit together. But I'm human. And like you, I struggle with things.

One afternoon a few years ago, I nearly broke down in tears while having coffee with a friend. Instead of wearing my normally brave face, I talked about how I really felt that day. It was hard, and it made me feel really uncomfortable. But you know what? From that point on, I felt a lot closer to this friend. That's the magic of vulnerability. It opens us up to experiencing each other more fully.

SPEAK UP FOR YOURSELF

One way we can be more true to ourselves is by speaking up for ourselves and our needs. But to do this successfully, we first need to *understand* our needs. This means separating our wants and needs to determine what really matters most to us. Then, we need to learn how communicate these needs so that we can get them met.

Identify Your Needs

Our core needs include feelings of competence, relatedness, and autonomy (Reis et al. 2000). Competence refers to feeling like we can take action effectively to improve ourselves and our skills. For example, we feel competent when we're good at something. We could be good at anything from baking to playing an instrument. Relatedness refers to feeling connected to others. To feel a sense of relatedness, we can't just be around other people. We have to feel cared for or close to people in some way. Autonomy refers to the feeling that we're the ones making the final decisions about our lives and actions. We can often feel a lack of autonomy when we feel others—like a parent, a spouse, or a boss— are choosing for us how we should live. Getting these three needs met is essential to our happiness (Ryan and Deci 2002).

Take a moment now to reflect on these three needs: competence, relatedness, and autonomy. In your notebook, rank each need on a scale from one (low) to ten (high) on how well you think each need is being met. Then, for each need, see if you can identify situations, people, or personal beliefs that are preventing you from getting the need met. For example, if you're feeling a lack of competence, is it because your job is really easy and repetitive? Sure, you might be good at it, but because it's so easy for you, it might not make you feel very competent. Or, maybe you're feeling a lack of competence because your romantic partner is always criticizing or nitpicking you. In this case, you might regularly feel like you can never do well enough to please your partner. The goal here is to figure out *why* you aren't getting your needs met.

If you're feeling a lack of relatedness, maybe it's simply because you spend a lot of time alone using your phone. Or maybe it's because you're not feeling *meaningfully* connected to your partner, friends, or coworkers. And if you're not feeling a sense of autonomy, it could be because your boss makes the decisions regarding every detail of your work—what to do, when to do it, and how to do it. A similar dynamic is common in relationships where one person feels a lack of autonomy because the other person decides everything, from where they live, to what they do, to who they see. These are just a few common examples of situations that can thwart our core needs.

One you've had a chance to reflect on whether your core needs are being met, write down three things you could do to get these needs met. For example, you may need to talk openly and honestly to the people who you feel are thwarting your needs. Often, the actions we need to take to get our needs met involve speaking up for ourselves. Not just once, but many times, as we continue to make our needs clear to ourselves and others. It's not that it's their job to meet our needs. But it's our job to communicate our needs and make the required changes in our lives to get those needs met.

Unfortunately, some people may not be able to accommodate your needs. They are humans too and are dealing with their own challenges. In the spirit of vulnerability, I'll share a personal example. I can be highly critical, and it has taken me time and effort to stop thwarting my partner's sense of competence with excessive criticism. In exchange for my effort, my partner has put more effort into planning activities that help me feel a greater sense of relatedness with him. We're doing great now. But there was a time in our marriage when we decided that if we continued to thwart each other's needs, then we needed to separate. That's because needs are so crucial to our happiness that when they are not met, happiness feels impossible.

So finally, ask yourself, "What will you do if other people are unable or unwilling to work with you to get your needs met?" Write your thoughts down in your notebook. If you effectively communicate your needs a few times, give people some time, and yet there is still no change, what will you do? Will you quit the job, the relationship, or the friendship? It sucks having to make these difficult decisions, but if we choose to stay in situations that thwart our needs, it's going to be pretty tough to be happy.

When I first started this process, I found out my work was thwarting my need for autonomy. But there was still a part of me that didn't think I *deserved* to get my needs met, and I didn't know how to communicate them. So, I just started slow. A little at a time, I started pushing back at work when I was asked to do things that went against my values. For example, when I was asked to use ethically questionable practices, I offered an alternate solution. And when asked to focus on projects that weren't meaningful for me, I requested other projects. At the same time, I continued to do the tasks that were required of me.

Now, I'll be honest. Speaking up for myself was super uncomfortable. But a funny thing happened. Just by standing up for myself, I started to feel a greater sense of self-worth. It felt like I had been waiting for someone to come along and stand up for me—all the while feeling like a victim. I didn't realize that the only person who could really stand up for me was me. Then, when I finally stood up for myself, I started to realize that my needs *were* worth fighting for, that I was worth fighting for. I didn't have to do things that made me feel bad about myself.

So what happened? Honestly, the more I tried to get my needs met at work, the worse things seemed to get. There was just no way for me to live my values and maintain a sense of autonomy at this particular job. But I least I knew that. I started networking and building new skills to find another job that was a better fit. And after leaving that job, I immediately started feeling a lot better. Sometimes we have to go through the suck to positively change our lives even if we don't yet know what the outcome will be.

Get Your Needs Met

So now that you know what your needs are, how do you communicate them so that you can get your needs met? To do this successfully, you have to be assertive: firm, but not hostile. The goal is to use "I" statements that represent your point of view without using "you" statements, which put all the emphasis on what the other person is doing wrong. For example, instead of hollering at your partner, "Why don't you ever look at me when I'm talking to you?" you could say, "I feel bad when I speak to you and you don't look up from your cellphone." Or instead of snapping at your boss, "Stop hovering over my computer. You're making me nervous!" You could say "I'd like to try this on my own. I'll come to you if I need help." Each of these statements expresses your feelings or desires instead of casting the blame on others. I know it sounds silly, but this simple trick makes other people way more willing to compromise with you because they aren't put on the defensive.

Try using these phrases to speak up for yourself more effectively:

- I notice that…

- I'm feeling _____. What are you feeling?

- I feel disappointed about _____.

- I would really like _____.

Learning to be assertive is key to effectively communicating your needs and getting them met. To practice assertiveness, choose one thing that you will say no to in the future and create a plan for how you will say no. Choose something that someone is likely to ask you, something that you don't want to do but might normally say yes to anyway. For example, you might say no to a friend who asks to borrow things and never returns them. Or, you might say no to going to dinner with your in-laws if you know they're just going to put you down. Write this thing down in your notebook and try to be as detailed and specific as possible. Now sticking to it? That's the hard part.

To continue to build this skill, start by asking people for things you wouldn't normally ask for. For example, when you are grocery shopping, ask an employee to show you where something is. Or ask a friend to meet you at your house if you always go out of your way to meet them at their house.

For some of you, these practices might be easy. For others of us, myself included, these tasks are incredibly hard because we're not used to asking for anything, let alone big things like getting our needs met. For example, I almost always say yes when people ask me for a favor. About half of the time, I regret it. It's also really hard for me to ask people for things because I don't want to be a bother. So starting small and getting your brain comfortable with assertiveness can make it easier to communicate your needs.

It's also easier to start building this skill in messages rather than IRL. We have the time and space to respond thoughtfully instead of just instinctively blaming others or agreeing to something we don't want to do. So use technology as an aid here if you need to. Pause, ask yourself, "Do I really want to do this?" And then respond.

OPEN YOURSELF TO OTHERS

Let's face it. Life in the technology age is stressful. It turns out that stress, regardless of where it comes from, triggers us to form stronger social identities, for example, political, religious, or ideological identities. These days we can form stronger identifies online by joining groups or associating only with people like us. We form these identities instinctively as a way to develop social connections that help us better cope with our stress. And as a result, we *do* feel more connected; we are buffered from negative experiences and even view stressors as less threatening (Haslam and Reicher 2006). It feels good, and boy do we need it.

The problem we have to watch out for is that when we form stronger social identities, we can start to see "our people" as better than "not our people" (Tajfel 1982, 1970). Because we are all so hungry for social connection in the technology age, we seem to be doing this more and more. Instead of being open to those who are different from us, we are more prone to prejudicial and discriminatory behavior, and we are more likely to be on the receiving end of this behavior. This cycle—a cycle fueled by fear, stress, and loneliness—will continue to build if we allow it to, leaving us in a perpetual state of unhappiness. The only solution is to cultivate openness, empathy, and compassion.

In this step so far, you have been learning how to encourage others to be open to you. Equally important to this step is learning how to be open to others, because authenticity is a two-way street. The good news is that as you increasingly learn how to be yourself and communicate your needs, you'll likely intuitively realize that others also deserve the opportunity to be themselves. Still, we can accidentally thwart other people's self-expression, and so we need to develop skills like empathy and compassion to ensure our relationships are mutually satisfying—so we not only get our needs met, but we also can help others get their needs met. This is why opening yourself to others is a key part of this step.

Tear Down Your Walls

A colleague of mine recently told me that people regularly walk up to her on the street to compliment her hat, have a brief conversation, or just share a random thought. Indeed, I agreed that she is a really easy person to approach. It got me wondering, *What can we do to encourage people to be more open with us?*

The concept of openness has been around a long time. We know that people who are open tend to like to try different foods, do new things, and reevaluate their ideas and assumptions (McCrae 1987). They're innately curious and eager to learn. So how do we cultivate these characteristics, particularly when it comes to being open to others?

Well, we've all been hurt in our romantic relationships, friendships, and likely even by strangers. So most of us have built psychological walls to protect ourselves. We don't want to let people get too close in fear that we'll get hurt again, but these walls only lead us to feel isolated and lonely. To open ourselves to others, first, we have to tear down our walls.

We do this with a combination of curiosity, courage, and acceptance. Curiosity is key because people won't usually open up to us unless we invite them to. For example, we might ask questions, maintain eye contact, and smile as we attempt to deeply listen when others are talking (McKay, Davis, and Fanning 2009). This shows we are curious about what they have to say, and they'll be more likely to open up to us.

Courage is key because it can feel scary or uncomfortable being around others when they are expressing their true selves. Real humans are flawed and weird and imperfect. They have difficult emotions, just as you do, and they might share things with you that are hard to hear. So it takes courage to voluntarily dive into these experiences with another person. Remember, not everything that increases happiness and connection is fun.

Acceptance is key because when others open up to you, your first inclination may be to judge them. They might think differently than you, believe different things than you, or engage in behaviors that you find disturbing. But if you judge them instead of trying to understand them, they won't open up to you again. So practice tearing down your walls by staying curious, courageous, and accepting.

You can do this by reaching out to people online or IRL. Both targeted one-on-one exchanges and broadcasting (posting) can help you break down your walls. This type of social media use helps you build weak social ties into stronger ones, maintain social ties that would have otherwise ended, and enhance the bonds you already have with your inner circle. You may even feel connected to a larger community (Verduyn et al. 2017).

Develop Your Empathy Reflex

We live around people like us, we work with people like us, and we talk to people like us in person and online. We are in our own bubbles, as some people say. As a result, we have lost much of our ability to be empathetic—to look at the world through other people's eyes (Konrath 2012). Without this ability, we might feel less connected simply because we have a hard time feeling connected to anyone *different from us*. Luckily, we can learn how to be more empathetic and increase our opportunities for connection.

One way to start developing your empathy reflex is by watching videos that recount the experiences of people who are different from you. Next time you watch a video, take a moment to think about the situation from the character's point of view. See if you can put yourself in each person's shoes, see the world from their perspective, and understand what might be motivating them to do what they are doing. This is especially helpful if you can take the perspective of a villain, bad guy, or unlikeable character.

Even though Hollywood movies might have you believe otherwise, very few people do things that they *believe* are bad, even if *we* believe the things they do are bad. We all have our reasons and backstories. Understanding people's reasoning is a crucial part of empathy and being open to others as they are. Of course, it's harder for us to be empathetic when the other person does or believes things that go against our values. But if we build our empathy skills, we can start to connect better with everyone. It doesn't mean we have to agree with them or do anything we don't believe in.

Another way to practice empathy is with the "characters" in your real life. First, think of a friend who has gone or is going through a hard time. Second, think of someone whom you just totally don't get—you don't like them, you don't understand them, and maybe you don't really want to. Third, think of someone you disagree with politically. Note these three people down in your notebook.

Now, try to put yourself in each person's shoes and practice seeing the world from their perspective. For each person, ask yourself the following questions to help build your empathy skills.

- What might have happened in their past that could be motivating them to act as they do?

- What struggles might they have had that made them who they are?

- What might you be missing that would help you understand this person better?

It doesn't always feel good to empathize because it can feel inconsistent with our identity. We can end up feeling the negative emotions they are feeling, or we can end up feeling like we actually understand someone who we hate. These conflicting thoughts and emotions can be confusing, but going through this process is important for happiness, especially in the technology age. It helps build stronger social connections by allowing more openness between us and the people around us. And remember, building stronger social connections is just about the best thing we can do for our happiness.

FINAL THOUGHTS

When you push yourself to keep growing by learning more challenging skills, you are able to overcome stalls in your happiness. In the technology age, these challenging skills often involve being yourself, speaking up for yourself, and opening yourself to others. And although it's not easy, building these skills can help you take your happiness to the next level.

Beat the Hedonic Treadmill

Once you have built the skills in this book, it's almost certain that you'll be able to outsmart your smartphone and feel a boost in happiness…but for how long? After you've learned these skills, you'll inevitably reach the dreaded plateau, or you may even start to backslide, not feeling as good as you did when you first started the seven steps. This phenomenon is known as the "hedonic treadmill" (Diener, Lucas, and Scollon 2009). It means that we can do many things to increase our happiness—things that *do* work for a bit—but if we simply continue doing these same things over and over, they'll eventually lose their effectiveness. It can end up feeling like you are on a treadmill, forever running and not getting anywhere. Luckily, we can get off the hedonic treadmill and sustain our gains in happiness, even in the technology age, as long as we know what to do (Layous and Lyubomirsky 2012).

In this chapter, we'll talk about how to beat the hedonic treadmill to maintain your happiness. You can do this by pursuing happiness in more social ways, getting out of your comfort zone, and making happiness a part of your daily routine. By implementing these strategies, you'll set yourself up for ongoing success that will persist long after you've completely abandoned this book. As a result, the journey we've taken here together won't be forgotten; it'll be integrated into your life in ways that benefit you permanently.

In this chapter, you'll learn how to:

- build happiness with others

- get out of your comfort zone

- make happiness a part of your daily routine.

BUILD HAPPINESS WITH OTHERS

It turns out that we are happier doing just about everything with other people than we are doing those things alone (Killingsworth 2017). That means that we'll likely enjoy building our happiness more if we do it with others. And if we enjoy the process more, we'll be more likely to stick to it. So if we work to build our happiness with others, we'll not only have their support but also their camaraderie. So here are some strategies that can help you build happiness with others.

Get Friends Involved in Your Journey

One thing technology does well is it allows us to communicate with people who are not actually with us. It allows us to share and receive messages so we can support each other as we build our happiness. We can reach out to friends to share our gratitude or say a kind word. We can join a group that aims to do good in the world or offer advice to people who could benefit. But we can also recruit our friends (those who are interested anyway) to join us in activities that improve our relationship with technology and boost happiness.

One way to do this is by doing the #OutsmartYourSmartphone twenty-eight-day challenge with your friends. As you know, you've been given a bunch of different activities throughout this book to help change the way you use your smartphone—for example, taking mindful moments without using your phone or changing the settings on your phone so it doesn't wake you up in the middle of the night. To more easily outsmart your smartphone with your friends, I've compiled some of these activities into a simple, fun, twenty-eight-day challenge for you to share. To start this challenge, go to the page for this book at http://www.newharbinger.com/43492 to get the free accessories.

See who can complete the most days and discuss how it went on social media with the hash tag #OutsmartYourSmartphone. I especially encourage you to share this challenge with adults who appear to have unhealthy relationships with technology and young people, as they tend to struggle more with the problems technology creates

(Twenge 2015). A simple share can strengthen several of your skills—for example, it can promote meaningful connections, help you practice kindness, and make a positive impact in someone's life—all things that help you cultivate your happiness.

Another way to build your happiness with others is by creating an Outsmart Your Smartphone activity group, meet up, or gathering. Invite your friends, family, or other people in your community to meet up weekly for seven weeks (one week per step) for one to three hours (depending on the size of your group). Everyone in the group should aim to complete one step per week. When you get together as a group, take turns sharing what you did that week to outsmart your smartphone, what gave you the most trouble, and how you could better manage this challenge in the future. After each person shares, others might offer advice based on their own experiences with the activities that week. With your activity group, you might also discuss the activities in the #OutsmartYourSmartphone challenge or other strategies that you all used to outsmart your smartphones that week. Having a regularly planned time to both connect with people IRL and work on improving your relationship with your smartphone can help you make faster progress toward your happiness goals. For more ideas about what to include in your own Outsmart Your Smartphone activity group, check out http://www.berkeleywellbeing.com.

In addition to explicitly inviting people to outsmart their smartphone with you, you can nudge others along by asking them to participate in small acts that generate happiness for *you both*. For example, you could organize more social events with friends to do things like eat out, go to concerts, play sports, do crafts, see movies, catch a comedy show, and tons of other things. Try combining a variety of different happiness-boosting strategies to get more bang for your buck—for example by organizing a social event where you do something kind, get outdoors, and connect with your friends.

A friend of mine did this recently by organizing a trip with friends to help a nonprofit clear out brush in a potential fire zone. Another person I know organizes small groups of people go clean out the stalls at an animal shelter. As long as you're doing something that matters to you and you're doing it with others, it can generate happiness. And by creating these meaningful experiences for the people in our lives, we not only increase our happiness, we also increase theirs.

Might you also want to build happiness with friends who are far away? Well, you can do that too. For example, I don't know about you, but I love writing and receiving a handwritten piece of snail mail—a letter, postcard, or note from someone I care about. The moment I see handwriting on a postcard, I start to get giddy. When I read a hand-written message from a friend or distant family member, I am down-right delighted.

You can create this feeling of delight in someone else by writing your own letters or postcards to people who live far away. By doing so, you encourage them to do the same. So make it a habit to send birth-day cards, holiday cards, and congratulations cards to people you care about. And don't forget to let them know you'd love to hear from them too. This practice can generate small, but meaningful moments of happiness and social connection while simultaneously making your pursuit of happiness more social.

Solicit the Support of Strangers

For some of us, building our happiness is too personal to share with our friends or family. If this sounds like you, you may prefer *not* to invite your friends, family, or community to engage in the process with you. That's okay. But I still suggest you attempt to increase your happi-ness *with others* to help you make better progress.

The great thing about the Internet is that there are tons of virtual communities of people all working together toward similar goals—for example, goals like losing weight, building muscle, or coping with a chronic disease. In addition, you can also join the online community of folks trying to outsmart their smartphones (or create a group of your own on your favorite social media site!). Search for the #OutsmartYourSmartphone hash tag to learn from others and share what you're doing using the #OutsmartYourSmartphone hash tag so others can learn from you.

Another way to build your happiness skills with the support of strangers is to attend a course, workshop, or retreat. You can choose an experience focused on a particular happiness-boosting skill—like resilience or gratitude—or look for an experience that will help you disconnect from technology and reconnect with the things that generate happiness. These types of groups can help you reach your wellness goals because they often provide additional inspiration, ideas, and camaraderie. As a bonus, pursuing your happiness with others shows you that everyone struggles with happiness from time to time, you're not alone, and we're all in this together.

Finally, if you're still struggling to outsmart your smartphone, you may benefit from getting a coach who can guide you, challenge you, and encourage you. A coach not only provides social support but also guidance in navigating the challenges that new technology will inevitably create.

GET OUT OF YOUR COMFORT ZONE

Our attention is increasingly being eaten up by technology (Kushlev 2018). We barely notice that our time is being consumed not only by reading and writing texts and emails, but also perusing social media, reading the news, and watching videos in many, if not most, of our spare moments. We are giving these activities our attention. And even though we may not realize it, using our attention on these activities takes effort and energy (Baumeister and Heatherton 1996). We can easily end up with attention fatigue without really understanding why. A sort of chronic lethargy can emerge. We might not feel bad, exactly, but we sure don't feel good.

Some people believe that most of us walk around the world now with some level of attention fatigue. As a result, we have a hard time mentally stepping back from life to observe it, analyze it, or change it. We have a difficult time planning or sticking to the plans we *do* make.

We might feel more irritable. And, interestingly, we are less likely to help others as a result (Kaplan 1995). This is how attention fatigue can throw us into a downward spiral of unhappiness and why restoring our attention is key to maintaining our happiness. So how do we overcome attention fatigue? We need to take creative breaks from media and technology.

Have Restorative Experiences

As a first step to overcoming attention fatigue, we need to have restorative experiences. Restorative experiences are experiences that have three components: They are different from our normal routine, they are fascinating to some extent, and they fit your needs and interests (Kaplan 1995). Although many experiences could be restorative, it turns out that getting out into nature tends to work really well because it so easily satisfies these three requirements. For example, to get to nature, most of us have to step out of our daily routines. In nature, there are endless things to evoke fascination—trees, plants, animals, and other sights we are not used to seeing. And if we like nature, that's even better.

It might seem hard at first to find these experiences. *Who has the time, energy, or money to truly get away?* we might think. But you really *can* do a lot with what you have nearby. Taking a walk in a nearby park or spending an afternoon in a botanical or community garden seems to be enough to satisfy our need to "get away" and "experience fascination" (Kaplan 1995). But be sure to choose something that's a good fit for you, something that you'll enjoy. For example, I am personally fascinated by the idea that the food we eat just grows from the dirt. The smell of tomato plants calms me, and the act of picking and eating food directly from the plant is just about the most relaxing thing I can think of (Soga, Gaston, and Yamaura 2017). So a restorative place for me is a vegetable garden, but everybody is different.

If you're thinking that having the restorative experiences you need is going to be tough to fit into your life, I get it. I live in an apartment with no yard, balcony, or even windows that open. So it's hard for me

to get to the spaces that restore me. You too may have restorative challenges, like living in the middle of a city with no green space or parks.
Or you might work daylight hours and have to find ways to restore
yourself at night. It's not always easy. We often have to get creative. For
example, to get my restorative experiences, I'll sometimes walk to a
local community garden, look at a neighbor's garden, or even pick wild
fruit that grows all around my city. It's not a perfect fit, but it does help,
even if only in small ways.

What about you? Take a moment now to think about what kinds
of restorative experiences would be most interesting to you and write
these down in your notebook. Be sure to list several experiences you
could have in nature, but feel free to list other experiences too, particularly if you're not especially drawn to nature. For example, you
might try going to an art gallery, a car show, a pet shop, a pick-your-
own fruit farm, a musical event, or any number of other events that are
different, fascinating, and interesting to you.

Once you have your list, schedule a time to try a couple of these
experiences out. Spend at least ten to fifteen minutes in the restorative
environment (but the longer the better) and when you're done, reflect
on how it made you feel by writing in your notebook. Ideally, try a few
different experiences to see which ones work best for you. But keep in
mind that if you continue going to the same place, the benefits are
likely to decline, so make sure you have several restorative environ-
ments to choose from.

Get Creative

Not too long ago, I tested out a new happiness app—an app that
seemed like it had real potential to make an impact. In this app, each
day for a week or two, I recorded my happiness, my creativity, and a
bunch of other things including how well I ate, how active I was, and
how mindful I was. When I was done, the app told me which activities
were most related to my happiness. To my surprise, creativity was the
thing most linked to my happiness. On days when I was creative, I
tended to be happier.

Before this moment, I hadn't even considered that creativity could be used to increase happiness. But indeed, it turns out that creativity contributes to happiness and happiness contributes to creativity (Dolan and Metcalfe 2012). Creativity leads to happiness because it enables us to pursue our goals, solve problems, and generate ideas more effectively (Di Giacinto, Ferrante, and Vistocco 2007; Baas, De Dreu, and Nijstad 2008). It just makes us more effective at life. So how can you generate creativity in ways that help you build and maintain your happiness?

Create Your Life Portrait

A lot of us claim we are not creative. But what we usually mean is that we are not *artistically* talented. Luckily, we don't need to be artistically talented to be creative. Creativity is a process. It's not about producing a perfect product—it's quite the opposite. Creativity is about making messes and coloring outside of the lines. So yes, even *you* can be creative.

One way to be creative and also build your happiness is to create a life portrait (Khoury et al. 2013). You've probably heard of a self-portrait, which is usually a drawing or painting of you. A life portrait, on the other hand, is less self-focused. It focuses on everything around you—for example, the people, pets, locations, and objects that impact you. In college, I actually had to create a life portrait for a class. I included an avocado (to represent being a vegetarian), my favorite book, a photo from the time I spent in New Zealand, a necklace from my partner, and some cards that I thought were pretty. These were the things that mattered to me at the time.

By creating a life portrait, you engage your creativity while also activating mindfulness, social awareness, feelings of gratitude, and a sense of meaning. You are shifting your attention to the things in your life that matter to you for a period of time while you create the portrait. If it takes you just a couple minutes, a full afternoon, weeks, or months, creatively bringing your attention to the meaningful things in your life can help you generate more happiness. In addition, activating the "creative" parts of your brain, which includes different neurons than the "thinking" parts of your brain, may help further strengthen your happiness skills because the more *different* neurons that get used when building your happiness skills, the more likely these skills will stick.

To create a life portrait, take a moment now to list in your notebook the people, places, and things that impact you or are meaningful to you. Ask yourself, "What, if removed from your life, would make you feel like you lost part of yourself?" Try to come up with at least twenty things. These are the things that might go into your life portrait.

Next, collect the tangible things into a pile. Of course, you won't be able to collect your children or pets or your favorite restaurant into a pile. So, add pictures of these people and places to the pile. Use this pile of things as inspiration for a painting, drawing, or collage.

You can attempt to make your life portrait realistic, or you can make it abstract, for example, by drawing everything in cartoon style, making something oversized and other things undersized, or by using the wrong colors. The more creative you can be while drawing the things that matter to you, the better. It really doesn't matter how it comes out—you can always throw away the final drawing if you don't like it. The goal is not to produce a work of art; the goal is to be creative while reflecting on what matters to you.

Alternatively, if you prefer to make a collage, you could use the pictures of everything on your list. Snap a photo of each of the people, places, and things, and combine all the photos together in a slide, document, or computer program. Arrange them however you like, creating a collage of things that matter to you. If you want to, do what I do: save the collage as a picture and set it to be your desktop background for continued inspiration throughout the day.

This activity can be used again and again as a strategy to reconnect with what's important to you and maintain your happiness. For example, over the years I've explored a number of topics with art just to figure out how I really felt about them—topics including positivity, self-harm, abortion, forest fires, and even politics. In each of these pieces, I just put paint on canvas or paper, not really worrying about how it would come out. The goal is just to explore your thoughts and feelings visually, a practice that takes us out of constantly trying to *think* our way to happiness. I know it can be hard, but this approach can help us discover parts of ourselves that are not easily accessible using our thoughts alone. So give this strategy a try.

Make Art as a Group

Another way to make art that can be fun and motivating is by creating a group art piece. For example, every year on my birthday, I put out a big piece of paper, colored markers, construction paper, and glue so people can stop by and add their contribution to the piece. I also usually draw a few squiggles and glue something first so that people don't feel weird about being the first person to add something.

This type of art—which I call a "Chester Picture," named after the family friend Chester who taught me this technique—is a great way to create synchrony between a group of people. Each person has to work around what the other people are doing, navigating their own space and the space that belongs to others. It can also generate a sense of connection between the people in the group. As each person contributes to the whole, they become part of something bigger than just them, and a sense of cohesion and camaraderie emerges. The art can also be a starting point for conversation, helping people who are less social or less familiar with the other people in the group to feel more socially connected.

Chester Pictures can be done with as few as two people to many thousands. In my city, there was recently a blackboard installed where hundreds of passersby contributed their thoughts, quotes, and pictures to a Chester Picture. So as you can see, there are many ways to generate happiness creatively.

Take a moment now to think about how you could try out a Chester Picture in your life. Would you ask a friend to make a drawing with you over coffee? Or would you set up an event that includes a larger group? Or would you try to create something even bigger, working with your local community to create a space for everyone in town to contribute? Take a moment now to reflect on this in your notebook and schedule a time in your calendar to try this activity out.

Make a Vision Board

Professional psychologists often balk at the idea of making a vision board. Indeed, the vision board is a commonly misused tool that some suggest will magically lead you to manifest all your goals and dreams. Of course, there is no magic when it comes to building your happiness. Still, there *is* value in making a vision board—an artistic work that helps you clarify what are your goals, dreams, and visions for the future.

To create a vision board, think about what your goals are, not only for your happiness but for your life. Try to avoid superficial goals like, "I want a nice car" or a "big house" or a "good job." These things are fine, but I want you to go a little deeper. If you want these things, think about *why* you want them. What does a nice car or big house or good job represent to you? Are you seeking a sense of security that you believe a nice home would provide to you? Are you seeking a feeling of respect that you believe a nice car would give you? Are you seeking to be a good caretaker for your loved ones and a good job would enable you to do this? Our real goals and dreams are not material objects; our real dreams are emotional and value-driven. That's why figuring out the emotions or experiences we want is key to achieving what we desire.

To prepare to make a vision board, take a moment now to write your dreams and goals in your notebook. For each thing you list, ask yourself, "Why?" a few times so see if you can find the deepest root of what you actually desire. For example: Why do you want to outsmart your smartphone? Are you feeling lonely? Do you feel like you're not spending your life how you really want? Why does this (and your other goals) actually matter to you? As you are writing, don't worry if you feel like you haven't quite gotten to the bottom of your goals and dreams. A vision board is meant to be a living document, so you can change and update it any time.

Once you have your list of goals, get a piece of paper, cardboard, poster board, or whatever else you have handy. Write your goals and feelings on different sections of the vision board. Leave room to attach pictures, cutouts from magazines, and other mementos, like receipts or sticky notes, if you choose. Add in whatever else you need to accurately represent the goals you have set for yourself. It's really up to you.

Just as an example, when I did this activity, it turned out that my goals all fit within four themes: my health, my career, my marriage, and my other social relationships. So I just wrote one thing in each quadrant of the piece of paper. Then I added all the goals and dreams I had related to these goals. For example, in my career quadrant, I have "write a book." In my marriage quadrant, I have "communicate kindly." And in my health quadrant, I have "grow a veggie garden." I have not yet achieved all these things, but the vision board reminds me of what's important to me so I don't lose track of where I want to go. It can help you stay on track too.

You may also want to include your values (from step 5) somewhere on your vision board because you want to ensure that you pursue your dreams in ways that are congruent with your values. If at any point, you notice you have written something on your vision board that doesn't fit with your values, I encourage you to cross it out. It's likely not going to feel good to pursue a goal that doesn't fit your values.

For example, on my vision board, I initially wrote down a weight loss goal I had. I kept trying to convince myself that this was consistent with my value of health. But every time I dieted, calorie-counted, and did extra exercise to lose weight, I always felt less healthy, both emotionally and physically. So losing weight was actually inconsistent with my values. Eventually, I figured this out. I then crossed out my weight loss goal and wrote "love yourself" instead. Now I aim to treat my body as well as I can, regardless of how it affects my weight. And it feels much better. These small changes in the goals we set for ourselves can make a surprisingly large impact on our happiness.

As you are creating your vision board, keep in mind that it will be the most effective if it guides you in living the kind of life *you* want to live—the kind of life where you live your values, satisfy your emotional needs, and pursue what matters *to you*. So give it a shot and see if this activity helps you better maintain your happiness longer term.

MAKE HAPPINESS PART OF YOUR DAILY ROUTINE

Take a moment to think about the last time you learned a new skill—maybe you learned how to speak a new language, play an instrument, or build a website. How long did it take you? How many total hours did you spend until you got good at it?

If you are an average human being, learning any new skill will take you some time. Happiness is no different because it takes time to rewire the connections in your brain. You wouldn't expect to lose fifty pounds in a week, and you shouldn't expect to increase happiness in a week either. To hardwire happiness skills in your brain—to make them as easy as adding two plus two or riding a bike—you must continue to practice your happiness skills again and again, even after you finish this book. Here are some tools to keep you on track.

Prioritize the Right Skills

To prioritize the right skills moving forward, take the Outsmart Your Smartphone Quiz again.

Please answer the following questions honestly. The purpose of taking this quiz again is to help you identify which of the skills in this book you still need to work on to outsmart your smartphone and build your happiness. A downloadable version of the quiz is available at http://www.newharbinger.com/43492.

Outsmart Your Smartphone Quiz

Rate the following statements honestly using a scale of 1 to 10, where 1 means strongly disagree and 10 means strongly agree.

Strongly disagree   Strongly agree

1   2   3   4   5   6   7   8   9   10

Step One: Build Foundational Skills

Skill	Statement	Rating
Growth Mindset	*I'm unable to improve my relationship with my phone.*	
Balance	*I use my phone during times I have set aside to relax.*	
Supportive Systems	*I rarely use my phone in ways that help me reach my goals.*	

Step Two: Stay Present

Skill	Statement	Rating
Fear of Missing Out	*I feel anxious when I don't have my phone nearby.*	
Technology Timeouts	*I have a hard time taking breaks from my phone or the Internet.*	
Mindful Moments	*I pull out my phone during many of my spare moments.*	

Step Three: Make Meaningful Connections

Skill	Statement	Rating
Strong Relationships	*I check my phone while spending time with friends or family.*	
Focus on Others	*I focus mostly on myself (my pictures, posts, and pages) when I'm online.*	

Skill	Statement	Rating
Communicate Kindly	I sometimes say mean things in messages, posts, or responses.	

Step Four: Manage Your Emotions

Skill	Statement	Rating
Self-Compassion	I feel bad about myself either in real life or online.	
Positivity	I have a hard time thinking positively about my life.	
Resilience	I struggle to recover from challenges, obstacles, or upsetting experiences.	

Step Five: Practice Kindness

Skill	Statement	Rating
Live Your Values	I struggle to understand or live my values.	
Find Your Purpose	I'm not sure what gives my life meaning or purpose.	
Make Positive Impacts	I rarely help others in ways that make me feel good.	

Step Six: Be True to Yourself

Skill	Statement	Rating
Be Yourself	It's hard for me to show my faults, fears, and insecurities either online or offline.	
Speak Up for Yourself	I struggle to tell others what I need from them to be happy.	
Open Yourself to Others	I have a hard time accepting people who are different from me.	

Step Seven: Beat the Hedonic Treadmill

Skill	Statement	Rating
Build Happiness with Others	*Anytime I pursue happiness, I do so alone, online, or on my phone.*	
Get Out of Your Comfort Zone	*I rarely try new things or get out of my comfort zone.*	
Make Happiness a Part of Your Daily Routine	*I have not really made happiness a priority in my life.*	

Look over your answers and write down the skill you scored lowest on in your notebook (your weak skill). Now, look over each skill in the quiz and write down the skill you most enjoyed building while reading this book (your strong skill). Feel free to look back over the steps to get a sense for which activities were for which skill. For the next month, your goal will be to work on building just these *two* skills (your weak skill and your strong skill). By focusing on just a couple of skills at a time, especially skills that are challenging or enjoyable for us, we are likely to make better progress than if we tried to do everything all at once. This way, we're not too bored, and we don't stretch ourselves too thin.

Now that you have your two skills to work on, take a moment to schedule when you'll do these activities in your calendar. Plan to work on these skills for a month, as often as you have time for. Working on them even a tiny bit is better than not doing anything at all. And be sure to set up email or text reminders if you think you might forget to stick to your plan.

Now, set up a reminder in your calendar to notify you once per month to prioritize *new* skills. When you get this reminder, repeat the process in this section to prioritize new skills. More specifically, take the quiz again, find a weak skill and a strong skill, and set up your monthly plan to build these skills. Each time you take the quiz, you'll see how much you've improved and switch to focusing on two new skills (or the same skills if they still need more work). Keep cycling through this process until you're satisfied with your relationship with your phone and other technology. Keep in mind that no relationship is perfect (even the one we have with our phone), but if you stick to this process, you *can* outsmart your smartphone.

Note that if you stop using the skills you've learned here, they will fade. If you don't use it, you may lose it. Just as reverting back to an unhealthy diet would likely lead you to regain weight that was lost, reverting back to unhealthy thoughts, emotions, and behaviors will again give your smartphone the opportunity to outsmart you.

On the flip side, the longer you practice these skills, the more they'll become automatic and the less frequently you'll have to set aside time to practice them. For example, instead of setting aside time to write gratitude notes to people on social media, you'll just feel grateful and express it without really having to think about it. Or, instead of having to set aside time for mindful moments, you'll just stay present and won't be compelled to pull out your phone. You won't have to *try* so hard to be positive, kind, or resilient—you will just be these things. All it takes is time and effort, and soon enough, you'll start to rewire your brain in the ways that make you happy.

Apply the Skills You Learned in Your Real Life

Now that you have your plan for the future, let's make happiness part of your routine. Throughout this book, you've engaged in a variety of activities, some of which you completed in your notebook and others you completed in your daily life. Although it can be really helpful to start building your happiness by reading books and doing written activities, the goal is to increasingly apply the skills you've learned in your daily life. For example, instead of writing your values down in your notebook, you should increasingly strive to live your values as you go about your daily routine.

This shift from building the happiness skills to applying the happiness skills is key to your success for a couple of reasons. First, we get busy or bored and often will end up skimping on the time we have devoted to building our happiness skills. No judgment from me; this is just human nature. Second, we often get better bang for our buck when we use these skills in our real life (versus just doing the activities in our notebook). So the sooner you start applying these skills, the better.

To apply any of the skills you learned in this book, start integrating them into your daily life. For example, you could apply your gratitude skills while grocery shopping—ask yourself, "What are you grateful for in this moment?" You could be more mindful on your walk to work—ask yourself, "What do you see, smell, hear, and feel as you take each step?" You could plan to do something kind for someone at work each Monday or plan to do volunteer work (like writing postcards for a political candidate) while grabbing drinks or dinner with friends. The goal is to wean yourself off the writing and thought exercises in this book and find ways to make the happiness skills a part of your everyday routine—go from *learning* it to *living* it.

Another trick to making these skills a part of your routine is by adding "reminder objects" to your environment. For example, you could put positive notes on your computer screen, put reminders on the fridge to reach out to friends, or leave your box of pens out to remind you to do creative happiness-building activities. Leave reminder objects anywhere that you go frequently—your home, work, desk, car, and phone—so you get reminded to do the things that generate happiness.

Celebrate Your Successes

We have this bad habit of continually downplaying our successes and not fully appreciating our efforts, small successes, and wins. For example, we may say, "Anyone could write a thank-you note to a friend," or "I didn't increase my happiness as much I wanted to." But this fails to recognize the effort that you put in—effort that not everyone would put in, believe me. And, these phrases minimize your success instead of celebrating it.

Did you notice a point increase on the quiz since the last time you took it? Give yourself a pat on the back. Did you make a positive impact in someone else's life with your kind words, a note of gratitude, or volunteering? Appreciate yourself for doing what, let's face it, a lot of people these days are not willing to do. The fact that you even made it here, to the end of step seven, shows that you're *really* trying, and that means way more than you realize. You rock, and don't forget it!

FINAL THOUGHTS

To beat the hedonic treadmill, keep up the variety. Build skills that are creative, fun, and social, and you'll more easily make gains in your happiness and maintain the happiness you've generated so far, even in the technology age. If you continue to rely on the seven steps and put these steps together in ways that work for you, you really can outsmart your smartphone and experience true happiness.

The Future of Happiness

Congratulations on completing the seven steps! If you have followed these steps and done many of the activities, it is very likely that you now know how to outsmart your smartphone and are feeling a bit happier than you were at the beginning of this book. But it is also likely that you're still not as happy as you want to be. That's because it takes time, effort, and consistency to build the life you really want. You'll come across new and different challenges, so you'll have to apply the skills you learned in new ways. And you'll have to do all this while living a world that is becoming *more* technology obsessed, not less.

As a society, we are just now realizing the huge impacts technology has on our happiness. As a result, people are finally starting to consider the relationship between technology and happiness more seriously. Existing technologies are being modified to try to shift more toward increasing happiness. Other technologies are designed specially to increase happiness. And society as a whole is even starting to focus more on happiness as a metric for success. So what will it take to maintain our happiness in the even more technology-dominated world of the future?

In this chapter, we'll talk about:

- the limits of technology

- where technology is headed

- creating a happier society.

THE LIMITS OF TECHNOLOGY

I'm one of those weird "old Millennials" who doesn't quite fit in either the millennial generation or Generation X. Like Generation Xers, I was a "latchkey kid"—a child who spent most of my childhood home alone in front of the TV while my parents were at work. But like Millennials, I was a digital native—a child who grew up alongside the Internet. In fact, the multicolored Apple logo on my parents' first computer is one of the very first images I remember from my childhood.

Looking back, it seems my childhood years, the 80s and 90s, just may have been the golden years of healthy technology. My friends and I would get together IRL to play computer games, go to chat rooms, and play video games. These were social experiences that brought us closer together and gave us a wonderful sense of social connection. Back then technology connected us. But then...technology changed.

Social media and smartphones seemed to shift us from technology that connected us to technology that disconnected us. People started turning away from intimate conversations to answer texts. They turned away from playing games together to playing games alone on their phones. And now, our smartphones are within reach (and often in view) nearly every moment of our lives. Technology is no longer bringing us together; it's tearing us apart.

The research is starting to pile up. Social media is hurting our well-being (Verduyn et al. 2017; Tandoc, Ferrucci, and Duffy 2015; Steers, Wickham, and Acitelli 2014). And it doesn't seem to matter which type of social media. For example, in one study, people reported that Facebook, Instagram, Twitter, and Snapchat all made them feel more depressed (Royal Society of Public Health 2017).

At the same time, smartphones are messing with our ability to enjoy our lives and each other (Dwyer, Kushlev, and Dunn 2017). When our smartphones are present, we have crappier interactions with each other (Brown, Manago, and Trimble 2016; Przybylski and Weinstein 2013), and we actually enjoy our real-life experiences less (Dwyer, Kushlev, and Dunn 2017).

But there is just no way we're quitting our smartphones (or other technology) any time soon. So instead of being anti-technology, it seems to me that a more realistic solution to these problems is to *prioritize* happiness more and change the impact our technology-driven world has on us. Some of that responsibility falls on us. And the majority of this book has been about what you can do to better manage your relationship with technology. But some of that responsibility should fall on the companies that develop technology. They also have an important role to play in helping us outsmart our smartphones and resist the temptation of toxic technologies.

Making Existing Technology More Positive

One of the ways that technology companies can prioritize happiness is with the design (or redesign) of their websites, platforms, apps, and so forth. Social media, for example, uses algorithms to choose posts that are most likely to get you to either click, stay on the site, or purchase something. As a result, many of the posts you see are the ones that get you the most riled up—you stay engaged, but not happy. Instead, algorithms could easily be programed to prioritize other things like connection, laughter, or gratitude. Maybe one day, these algorithms will be optimized to show you the posts that are most likely to make you laugh, help you connect, or even make a positive change IRL. But until this happens, it's up to us to avoid social media that makes us feel bad.

Another way that technology companies can prioritize happiness is with the tools or features they provide you. For example, the default settings on smartphones could be set to optimize your happiness. Notifications could be limited; harmful apps (like social media) could use grayscale icons or be in folders that are harder to get to; apps that improve happiness, sleep, nutrition, and exercise could be pre-installed. Lucky for us, both Google and Apple are already working on digital well-being tools, so you can now get some of this on most smartphones. With such rapid advances in technology, I expect that these tools will continue to improve quickly.

Although technology companies have many opportunities to redesign their apps and products to better promote happiness, keep in mind that there are few incentives for them to make major changes, particularly if these changes negatively affect the bottom line. Why would a technology company prioritize your happiness when it makes more money from keeping you angry, clicking, and buying? Maybe one day our technologies will no longer hurt our happiness, but in the meantime, we'll have to take our happiness into our own hands, for example by minimizing our use of technology when possible, choosing to use websites that don't make us feel bad, and using the skills we've learned in this book to have more positive experiences when we're online.

Making New Happiness-Boosting Technologies

In addition to making existing technologies more positive, businesses can also make new technologies with the explicit purpose of increasing happiness. As we discussed earlier in this book, many of these technologies already exist. For example, there are apps that merge happiness skill building with online games. Still other apps provide text-based or video-based therapy. There are even emotion-sensing wristbands. Unfortunately, there are currently a lot of problems with many of these technologies.

Problems with Happiness-Boosting Technologies

So that you have a better sense of which happiness-boosting technologies to use and avoid, here's an overview of some of the problems.

One size does not fit all. At this point, most happiness-boosting technologies are being sold to you through one-size-fits-all marketing. They say: if you do this one thing—mindfulness, gratitude, or whatever—you will be happier. But the truth is that it's actually super important that you discover and choose happiness-boosting activities that work *for you*. It is only when you find the activities that you like, and therefore are willing to do, that happiness will start to come more easily.

Unfortunately, at the moment, the majority of these technologies do very little to help you identify what works best for you. So, you do the activities that you're told to do, end up no happier, and possibly even blame yourself rather than the technology that was poorly designed.

Self-focus is not the best route to happiness. Some happiness-boosting technologies take you in the complete wrong direction without even realizing it. How? By asking you to reflect on your experiences too much—for example by having you track your emotions, experiences, or thoughts daily. It turns out that the more we think about how we feel and why we feel that way, the less enjoyable our experiences can become (Nolen-Hoeksema and Morrow 1991). At best, tracking our experiences interrupts our ability to be present in the moment, fragmenting our attention, and dampening positive emotions. For those of us who might be a bit more neurotic, tracking experiences could even send us into a full-on downward spiral: *Why am I not happy? It must be because there is something wrong with me. I'll never be happy*...and so on.

Spending more time alone is not good for happiness. Another big problem with happiness-boosting technologies is that they might lead you to spend more time alone, "working on your happiness" on your phone or computer. If you're spending more time alone, your happiness-building efforts are taking you away from your social life. Because connecting with others is likely one of the best ways to increase happiness, using these technologies may potentially harm your happiness in the long-run rather than helping it.

Happiness comes not from within us, but from the space between us. As you learned in the very beginning of this book, many of the causes of our unhappiness are outside of us—in our workplace, our community, and our culture. Simply delivering advice for how to help *yourself* does not even come close to being a complete solution for fixing your happiness. Particularly given that current happiness-boosting technologies have you focus almost exclusively on yourself (rather than others), you are unlikely to see significant changes in your happiness as a result of using them.

Increasing Happiness with Technology

Although few technologies do much to help us outsmart our smartphone or increase our happiness, they are slowly getting better. More scientists are joining up with app developers, and greater efforts are being made to make sure that technologies designed to boost happiness actually *do* boost happiness. As a result of these new efforts, tech-based solutions for unhappiness are likely to continue improving in the near future.

One way this is likely to happen is with use of algorithms to personalize your happiness journey. We currently see the success of algorithms if we look just about everywhere. They determine which videos are recommended on streaming services, which content we should read on social media and news sites, and which ads we should see all over the web. But algorithms can also be used to recommend happiness skills you need to build or strategies you can use to improve your relationship with technology. And these types of algorithms are starting to be used more and more.

How do these algorithms work? Well, the technologies we use currently (like smartphones) collect tons of data on us—like where we go, what we like, and what we search for online. All this data has implications for our health and happiness. For example, one company looks at your movement throughout the day, call patterns, and text patterns—all data collected on your phone—to detect potential mental health issues and automatically notify a third party. Technologies like these that use data to identify issues and provide solutions can potentially revolutionize the way we go about increasing our happiness and well-being. So even though I've aimed to write this book in ways that help you build the skills that are most helpful *for you*—for example by focusing on the most important skills, your weaker skills, and skills that are more fun—algorithms will soon be able to do this way better than any book, including this one!

But, algorithms are just the first part of technologies that will help you on your personalized happiness journey. When these algorithms are eventually combined with well-designed and evidence-based content (like the content from this book), they'll not only know what you need, they'll be able to deliver it right to you, when you need it. For example, an algorithm may be able to detect that you're struggling with positive thinking and that this is hurting your happiness. In order for this algorithm to improve your life, it also needs to be able to provide you with the best and most effective solution to your problem. This is where I see technology and the science of happiness coming together to make real, positive impacts in our lives. When these technologies are eventually developed, you'll spend less time trying things that don't actually increase your happiness and less time building skills you don't really need. As a result, you'll be able to increase your happiness faster and more effectively.

WHERE SHOULD TECHNOLOGY GO NEXT?

In addition to the types of technology being created today to build happiness, there are many other possibilities that are yet to be explored. Some of these things could be done right away and make a huge impact. For example, the principles in the book could be applied to the development of *all* technologies. So instead of websites giving you content to keep you clicking more, reading longer, or buying more, websites could be optimized for happiness—your happiness, community happiness, and global happiness. I'm not saying that this would be an easy task, but I do believe it's possible and worth doing.

Implementing the principles of this book into *existing* technologies may be even easier. For example, think about when you're on hold, waiting for a customer service person and you're listening to that annoying music that plays over and over again until you just want to scream. That does nothing to ease your anger and anxiety and certainly doesn't make the service person's job any easier. What if instead, we heard a mindfulness meditation tape when we were on hold? We'd practice mindfulness while we wait, hopefully becoming calmer rather than more riled up and possibly even have a better interaction with the customer service person.

Or, what if we could download a virtual cartoon character to our desktop to keep us company throughout the day. It could periodically share inspirational messages, tell us jokes, or give us reminders to think of something we're grateful for. By delegating the job of building our happiness to technology, we can save our limited brain space for the zillion other things we have to do, and still increase our happiness.

Or, what if there was a website where we could review all major websites, sharing our feedback on how these websites make us *feel*— basically it could be what Yelp is to restaurants or Glassdoor is to jobs. If we knew the emotions that different websites created, we might be more inclined to make better choices and interact more with websites that increase happiness instead of decrease it.

The point is that technology is not evil; it can even increase our happiness if designed correctly. But in order for this to happen, we all need to start prioritizing happiness when it comes to the technologies we choose to use. If we prioritize happiness, then technology companies, both existing and new ones, will work harder to give us what we want. As a result, we'll not only increase our own happiness, but the happiness of everyone else around us. That's how we, even as individuals, can increase happiness globally.

CREATING A HAPPIER SOCIETY

As we discussed in the very beginning of this book, the causes of unhappiness are both inside and outside of us. This is, in part, why so many of us struggle with unhappiness—we are affected not just by our own thoughts and behaviors, but also by what's happening in the world around us. Fortunately, we are starting to better understand how larger social and cultural factors influence our happiness, and as a result, some efforts are being made to improve happiness in larger groups rather than just individuals. Here are some blossoming trends that will hopefully lead to us experience greater happiness in the years to come.

Building Happiness at Work

A while back I was asked to chat with a bunch of students. The students, feeling relieved about finishing their final projects, were building up new anxiety in preparation for entering the job market, so we were discussing the recent trend for each job candidate to go through half a dozen interviews before being offered or denied a job. One student told me that one company required eleven interviews! To me, this sounds insane. But this company believed that doing *more* interviews would result in *better* hires. More is better, right? That makes sense intuitively. But is it actually true? Let's think about it.

Imagine you're interviewing with two great companies. At one company, you have to do eleven interviews; at the other, you only have to do two interviews. If both companies offered you the exact same position at the exact same pay, which company do you think you would choose? I don't know about you, but I'd be annoyed that I had to spend time preparing, taking time off from work, and stressing about eleven interviews. The company may know more about *me*, but I also know more about *them*. I know that they don't respect my time, they make slow decisions, and they likely don't know how to run their business efficiently. So I would choose the company where I did fewer interviews.

It turns out I'm not alone. Sixty-seven percent of job candidates start to feel negative about a company after just three rounds of interviews (Montage 2014; Greenfield 2015). So even though many companies believe that doing more interviews results in better hires, this approach usually pushes away the very best job candidates (Moldad 2017; Sullivan 2014) because it makes them *unhappy*.

This is just one example of how organizations currently make decisions without considering how these decisions affect people's happiness. For example, cutting pay and benefits, overworking and undervaluing employees, and neglecting to help people develop themselves and their careers are just some ways that organizations decrease their employees' happiness. These employees tend to pass on their unhappiness to customers, these organizations tend to be less successful, and even stockholders don't get the returns they hoped for. It turns out that prioritizing employee happiness is good for employees, good for customers, and good for the bottom line (Harter et al. 2009).

Luckily, science has proven this. So, many organizations are now coming to realize that building happiness among their employees is worth the effort. For example, workplace wellness programs might teach you how to eat better, exercise, and practice mindfulness to help you boost your well-being. Other workplace well-being programs focus on improving workplace culture—for example by improving work-life balance, providing better employee benefits, and training better managers. In the years to come, as the economy becomes increasingly competitive, we're likely to see more of these workplace wellness programs, and more of them are likely to be comprehensive, focusing on both skills that you can build as an individual and factors that improve the broader workplace culture. As a result, more of us are likely to become happier, one organization at a time.

In the meantime, if we do not work at one of these organizations, we *can* do small things to make a positive impact in our workplaces. We can be kind, giving, and supportive of the people we work with, using the skills we built throughout this book. To make an even bigger positive impact, you could talk to your boss or someone in your employer's human resources department about providing everyone access to an online happiness course. Remember, working to increase the happiness of those around you can provide great benefits, both for you and those you help.

Building Happiness in Communities

While some people are working on building happiness at work, other people are focusing on building happiness in communities.

Architects, city planners, artists, and regular folks like you and me are taking small steps to create communities that foster social connection, support, and generosity.

For example, some people design spaces that optimize happiness, often focusing on building social connections between community members. Houses can be built in groups with a shared park and barbeque pit in the center, leading to more social interaction and a greater sense of community. Common spaces, like water features, dog parks, and community gardens can be built to bring community members together for socializing and activities. And additional features, like chess boards, interactive sculptures, or graffiti walls, can be added to existing parks to stimulate social interactions between people in common spaces. Slowly, but surely, more attention is being paid to improving our cities and communities in ways that optimize our happiness.

Of course, you and I may not be so lucky as to live in one of these happiness-producing meccas. Luckily, we too can make small changes in our neighborhoods to improve happiness in our communities. One of my favorite ways to do this is by creating a Little Free Library. You can build a Little Free Library in your front yard by erecting what is essentially an oversized mailbox with a clear door. Stock it with books you no longer plan to read and leave a sign out that anyone is free to take or leave book in the box. There are nearly half of a dozen of these libraries in my neighborhood, and they help us communicate to each other that we want to support each other.

There are still tons of other things you can do to create happier communities. Some folks might engage and support their community by planting fruit trees, berry bushes, or vegetables on the patches of dirt between the sidewalk in front of their house and the street. This fresh food can be a resource for people in need as well as a fun place for kids to stop, learn, and play. In my experience, kids are absolutely enamored with the idea of picking things like berries and tomatoes. And as a bonus for us, seeing their little eyes light up can be quite delightful.

If you want to do a smaller community-building task, you could consider starting a neighborhood watch, shoveling snow off your neighbors' sidewalks, helping your neighbors take their trash to the curb, or raking leaves for elderly folks nearby. You could install a bench, chess board, or swing at the edge of your property for others to enjoy. Or you could even leave out a chalkboard where passersby can contribute their own words and pictures.

Another idea is to put up a yard sign with a positive message. These days, yard signs often highlight the ways in which we are different from each other—for example, by displaying our political preferences, religious preferences, or other group identification. What if instead we put up signs that demonstrated the ways we are united to others in our community? For example, you could make a sign with a picture of your funny cat (I mean who doesn't like funny cat pictures?!). You could post a quote or joke that people in your town will know or create a sign of support for a local business.

Even those of us who live in apartments can contribute to our communities by posting a sign in our window, offering to help a neighbor with their garden, or seeing if we can plant a fruit tree for everyone in the apartment building. The goal is for each of us to make our communities just a little bit more social, supportive, and bright. And if enough of us do just a few tiny things, our efforts will add up to something amazing.

Building Happiness in Countries

In the United States, we measure gross domestic product (GDP) to determine how well our country is doing. But even as GDP has risen, we have seen large increases in mental health issues, suicide, and drug abuse. This has led some to question if GDP is really the best way to measure the success of a country. Maybe happiness is what we should really strive for.

In an effort to better prioritize happiness, some countries are taking a different approach. For example, Bhutan has begun using Gross National Happiness (GNH) as an indicator of the nation's success (Schroeder 2018). And in recent years, GNH has been used in several other countries as well, including the United States.

Similarly, the World Happiness Report, a publication of the United Nations, has been working to identify the happiest countries, the causes of happiness, and policy implications. From this report, we see that income per capita has risen in America, yet both social support and healthy life expectancy have declined substantially (Sachs, Layard, and Helliwell 2018). And both of these declines are tied to happiness. Healthy life expectancy appears to be falling as a result of increased obesity, opioid addiction, and suicidality, all things related to unhappiness. And our social support appears to be falling because we are less connected to other people and to our social institutions, also things related to unhappiness. As a result of all these factors combined, Americans are actually less happy than many other countries, especially Northern European countries (Sachs, Layard, and Helliwell 2018).

What can we do to increase happiness in America? It can feel like a huge weight on our shoulders to change the culture of an entire nation. And indeed, each of us alone is likely to have very little impact on the social structures that affect happiness. But together, we actually can make real and substantial changes that vastly improve the lives of people across the country and even the globe. We do so one mindful moment, one connection, and one kind act at a time.

SO WHAT NOW?

People tell me all the time that they feel like something is missing from their lives. They can't quite put their finger on it, but when they describe to me what's missing, it is always the same thing: connection—connection to self, to others, to community, and to an infinite number of other small things that we can't even quite identify. We know intuitively that by connecting to the Internet on our phones, computers, and other devices, we're losing our ability to connect to the things that *really* matter.

So even though I'm not yet ready to give up on technology completely, maybe more technology *isn't* actually the best solution to the problems *caused* by technology. Rather, the best strategy for increasing happiness now, in the technology age, is to create real connections and real experiences with real human beings. When we do this, we can finally build happiness—the kind of happiness that we won't want to stop pursuing, the kind of happiness that no one could convince us to stop pursuing, the kind of happiness that lasts for life.

References

Aknin, L. B., E. W. Dunn, and M. I. Norton. 2012. "Happiness Runs in a Circular Motion: Evidence for a Positive Feedback Loop Between Prosocial Spending and Happiness." *Journal of Happiness Studies* 13 (2): 347–355.

Aknin, L. B., E. W. Dunn, A. V. Whillans, A. M. Grant, and M. I. Norton. 2013. "Making a Difference Matters: Impact Unlocks the Emotional Benefits of Prosocial Spending." *Journal of Economic Behavior and Organization* 88: 90–95. https://doi.org/10.1016/j.jebo.2013.01.008.

Anderson, L. N., M. Cotterchio, B. A. Boucher, and N. Kreiger. 2013. "Phytoestrogen Intake from Foods, During Adolescence and Adulthood, and Risk of Breast Cancer by Estrogen and Progesterone Receptor Tumor Subgroup Among Ontario Women." *International Journal of Cancer* 132 (7): 1683–1692.

Ayduk, Ö., and E. Kross. 2010. "From a Distance: Implications of Spontaneous Self-Distancing for Adaptive Self-Reflection." *Journal of Personality and Social Psychology* 98 (5): 809–829. http://doi.org/10.1037/a0019205.

Baas, M., K. W. De Dreu, and B. A. Nijstad. 2008. "A Meta-Analysis of 25 Years of Mood-Creativity Research: Hedonic Tone, Activation, or Regulatory Focus?" *Psychological Bulletin* 134 (6): 779.

Baker, Z. G., H. Krieger, and A. S. LeRoy. 2016. "Fear of Missing Out: Relationships with Depression, Mindfulness, and Physical Symptoms." *Translational Issues in Psychological Science* 2 (3): 275.

Barlett, C. P., C. L Vowels, and D. A. Saucier. 2008. "Meta-Analyses of the Effects of Media Images on Men's Body-Image Concerns." *Journal of Social and Clinical Psychology* 27 (3): 279–310.

Baumeister, R. F., and T. F. Heatherton. 1996. "Self-Regulation Failure: An Overview." *Psychological Inquiry* 7 (1): 1–15. http://doi.org/10.1207/s15327965pli0701_1.

Baumeister, R. F., K. D. Vohs, and D. M. Tice. 2007. "The Strength Model of Self-Control." *Current Directions in Psychological Science* 16 (6): 351–355.

Boehm, J. K., and S. Lyubomirsky. 2009. "The Promise of Sustainable Happiness." In *The Oxford Handbook of Positive Psychology*, 2nd ed. Edited by S. L. Lopez and C. R. Snyder. Oxford, England: Oxford University Press.

Bridges, A. J., R. Wosnitzer, E. Scharrer, C. Sun, and R. Liberman. 2010. "Aggression and Sexual Behavior in Best-Selling Pornography Videos: A Content Analysis Update." *Violence Against Women* 16 (10): 1065–1085.

Brown, G., A. M. Manago, and J. E. Trimble. 2016. "Tempted to Text: College Students' Mobile Phone Use During a Face-to-Face Interaction with a Close Friend." *Emerging Adulthood* 4 (6): 440–443.

Bruehlman-Senecal, E., and O. Ayduk. 2015. "This Too Shall Pass: Temporal Distance and the Regulation of Emotional Distress." *Journal of Personality and Social Psychology* 108 (2): 356.

Case, A., and A. Deaton. 2015. "Rising Morbidity and Mortality in Midlife Among White Non-Hispanic Americans in the 21st Century." *Proceedings of the National Academy of Sciences* 112 (49): 15078–15083.

Chapman, A. L., K. L. Gratz, and M. Z. Brown. 2006. "Solving the Puzzle of Deliberate Self-Harm: The Experiential Avoidance Model." *Behaviour Research and Therapy* 44 (3): 371–394. http://doi.org/10.1016/j.brat.2005.03.005.

Cohen, J., and G. Weimann. 2000. "Cultivation Revisited: Some Genres Have Some Effects on Some Viewers." *Communication Reports* 13 (2): 99–114.

Davis, T.. 2016. "Results from the Berkeley Well-Being Survey." Berkeley Well-Begin Institute, September 13. https://www.berkeleywellbeing.com/happiness-blog/results-from-the-berkeley-well-being-survey.

Davis, T. S., B. Q. Ford, M. Riese, K. McRae, P. Zarolia, E. Butler, and I. B. Mauss. 2013. "Look on the Bright Side: Effects of Positive Reappraisal Training on Psychological Health." Society for Personality and Social Psychology, Emotion Pre-Conference, New Orleans, LA.

Davis, T. S., I. B. Mauss, D. Lumian, A. S. Troy, A. J. Shallcross, P. Zarolia, B. Q. Ford, and K. McRae. 2014. "Emotional Reactivity and Emotion Regulation Among Adults with a History of Self-Harm: Laboratory Self-Report and Functional MRI Evidence." *Journal of Abnormal Psychology* 123 (3): 499–509. http://doi.org/10.1037/a0036962.

Desjarlais, M., and T. Willoughby. 2010. "A Longitudinal Study of the Relation Between Adolescent Boys and Girls' Computer Use with Friends and Friendship Quality: Support for the Social Compensation or the Rich-Get-Richer Hypothesis?" *Computers in Human Behavior* 26 (5): 896–905.

Di Giacinto, M., F. Ferrante, and D. Vistocco. 2007. "Creativity and Happiness." International Conference, Policy for Happiness, Siena, Certosa di Pontignano.

Dickler, J. 2017. "Most Americans Live Paycheck to Paycheck." CNBC, August 14. https://www.cnbc.com/2017/08/24/most-americans-live-paycheck-to-paycheck.html.

Diehl, K., G. Zauberman, and A. Barasch. 2016. "How Taking Photos Increases Enjoyment of Experiences." *Journal of Personality and Social Psychology* 111 (2): 119.

Diener, E., R. E. Lucas, and C. N. Scollon. 2009. "Beyond the Hedonic Treadmill: Revising the Adaptation Theory of Well-Being." In *The Science of Well-Being*, 103–118. Springer.

Dolan, P., and R. Metcalfe. 2012. "The Relationship Between Innovation and Subjective Wellbeing." *Research Policy* 41 (8): 1489–1498.

Duckworth, A. L., C. Peterson, M. D. Matthews, and D. R. Kelly. 2007. "Grit: Perseverance and Passion for Long-Term Goals." *Journal of Personality and Social Psychology* 92 (6): 1087.

Dunning, D. 2011. "The Dunning-Kruger Effect: On Being Ignorant of One's Own Ignorance." In *Advances in Experimental Social Psychology* edited by M. P Zanna, P. Devine, J. M. Olson, and A. Plant. Cambridge, MA: Academic Press.

Dweck, C. S. 2009. "Mindsets: Developing Talent Through a Growth Mindset." *Olympic Coach* 21 (1): 4–7.

Dwyer, R. J., K. Kushlev, and E. W. Dunn. 2017. "Smartphone Use Undermines Enjoyment of Face-to-Face Social Interactions." *Journal of Experimental Social Psychology* 78 223–239.

Emmons, R. A., and M. E. McCullough. 2003. "Counting Blessings Versus Burdens: An Experimental Investigation of Gratitude and Subjective Well-Being in Daily Life." *Journal of Personality and Social Psychology* 84 (2): 377–389.

Ferrie, J. E., M. J. Shipley, M. G. Marmot, S. A. Stansfeld, and G. D. Smith. 1998. "An Uncertain Future: The Health Effects of Threats to Employment Security in White-Collar Men and Women." *American Journal of Public Health* 88 (7): 1030–1036.

Fogg, B. J. 2009. "A Behavior Model for Persuasive Design." Proceedings of the 4th International Conference on Persuasive Technology.

Ford, B. Q., and I. B. Mauss. 2014. "The Paradoxical Effects of Pursuing Positive Emotion: When and Why Wanting to Feel Happy Backfires." In *The Light and Dark Side of Positive Emotion*, edited by J. Gruber and J. Moskowitz. Oxford, England: Oxford University Press.

Goffman, E. 1959. "The Presentation of Self in Everday Life." *Butler, Bodies that Matter*. New York: Anchor Books.

Greenfield, R. 2015. "Machines Are Better Than Humans at Hiring the Best Employees." *Bloomberg Business*, November 17.

Guest, A. M., and S. K. Wierzbicki. 1999. "Social Ties at the Neighborhood Level: Two Decades of GSS Evidence." *Urban Affairs Review* 35 (1): 92–111.

Guillory, J. E., J. T. Hancock, C. Woodruff, and J. Keilman. 2015. "Text Messaging Reduces Analgesic Requirements During Surgery." *Pain Medicine* 16 (4): 667–672. http://doi.org/10.1111/pme.12610.

Hagerty, M. R. 2000. "Social Comparisons of Income in One's Community: Evidence from National Surveys of Income and Happiness." *Journal of Personality and social Psychology* 78 (4): 764–771.

Haggans, C. J., A. M. Hutchins, B. A. Olson, W. Thomas, M. C. Martini, and J. L. Slavin. 1999. "Effect of Flaxseed Consumption on Urinary Estrogen Metabolites in Postmenopausal Women." *Nutrition and Cancer* 33 (2): 188–195.

Harter, J. K., F. L. Schmidt, E. A. Killham, and S. Agrawal. 2009. "Q12 Meta-Analysis: The Relationship Between Engagement at Work and Organizational Outcomes." Omaha, NE: Gallup.

Haslam, S. A., and S. Reicher. 2006. "Stressing the Group: Social Identity and the Unfolding Dynamics of Responses to Stress." *Journal of Applied Psychology* 91 (5): 1037–1052.

Holt-Lunstad, J., T. F. Robles, and D. A. Sbarra. 2017. "Advancing Social Connection as a Public Health Priority in the United States." *American Psychologist* 72 (6): 517–530.

Hayes, S. C., K. D. Strosahl, and K. G. Wilson. 2012. *Acceptance and Commitment Therapy.* New York: The Guilford Press.

Ingram, R. E. 1990. "Self-Focused Attention in Clinical Disorders: Review and a Conceptual Model." *Psychological Bulletin* 107 (2): 156–176.

Johnson, K. R., and B. M. Holmes. 2009. "Contradictory Messages: A Content Analysis of Hollywood-Produced Romantic Comedy Feature Films." *Communication Quarterly* 57 (3): 352–373.

Kaplan, S. 1995. "The Restorative Benefits of Nature: Toward an Integrative Framework." *Journal of Environmental Psychology* 15 (3): 169–182.

Kawachi, I., and L. F. Berkman. 2001. "Social Ties and Mental Health." *Journal of Urban Health* 78 (3): 458–467.

Keltner, D., and J. J. Gross. 1999. "Functional Accounts of Emotions." *Cognition and Emotion* 13 (5): 467–480.

Khoury, B., T. Lecomte, G. Fortin, M. Masse, P. Therien, V. Bouchard, M. Chapleau, K. Paquin, and S. G. Hofmann. 2013. "Mindfulness-Based Therapy: A Comprehensive Meta-Analysis." *Clinical Psychology Review* 33 (6): 763–771.

Killingsworth, M. 2017. "Track Your Happiness: Preliminar Results" (unpublished research presented at IPSR Colloquium, UC Berkeley).

Kim, J. 2014. "Mindfulness Meditation Training and Stress Reactivity: Behavioral Emotion Regulation Mechanisms." Honors Thesis, Carnegie Mellon University.

Konrath, S. 2012. "The Empathy Paradox: Increasing Disconnection in the Age of Increasing Connection." In *Handbook of Research on Technosel* edited by R. Luppicini. Hershey, PA: Information Science Reference.

Krasnova, H., H. Wenninger, T. Widjaja, and P. Buxmann. 2013. "Envy on Facebook: A Hidden Threat to Users' Life Satisfaction?" International Conference on Wirtschaftsinformatik, Lepzin Germany, February.

Kushlev, K. 2018. "Media Technology and Well-Being: A Complementarity-Interference Model." In *Handbook of Well-Being,* edited by S. Oishi, E. Diener, and L. Tay. Salt Lake City, UT: DEF Publishers.

Kushlev, K., and S. J. Heintzelman. 2017. "Put the Phone Down: Testing a Complement-Interfere Model of Computer-Mediated Communication in the Context of Face-to-Face Interactions." *Social Psychological and Personality Science* http://doi.org/10.1177.1948550617722199.

Kushlev, K., J. D. E. Proulx, and E. W. Dunn. 2017. "Digitally Connected, Socially Disconnected: The Effects of Relying on Technology Rather than Other People." *Computers in Human Behavior* 76: 68–74.

Layous, K., and S. Lyubomirsky. 2012. "The How, Who, What, When, and Why of Happiness: Mechanisms Underlying the Success of Positive Interventions." In *Light and Dark Side of Positive Emotion* edited by J. Gruber and J. Moskowitz. Oxford, England: Oxford University Press.

MacLeod, C., E. Rutherford, L. Campbell, G. Ebsworthy, and L. Holker. 2002. "Selective Attention and Emotional Vulnerability: Assessing the Causal Basis of Their Association Through the Experimental Manipulation of Attentional Bias." *Journal of Abnormal Psychology* 111 (1): 107–123.

Malhotra, A., T, Noakes, and St. Phinney. 2015. "It Is Time to Bust the Myth of Physical Inactivity and Obesity: You Cannot Outrun a Bad Diet." *British Association of Sport and Exercise Medicine* 49 (15): 967–968.

McCrae, R. R. 1987. "Creativity, Divergent Thinking, and Openness to Experience." *Journal of Personality and Social Psychology* 52 (6): 1258–1265.

McKay, M., Ma.Davis, and P. Fanning. 2009. *Messages: The Communication Skills Book*. Oakland, CA: New Harbinger Publications.

Mojtabai, R., M. Olfson, and B. Han. 2016. "National Trends in the Prevalence and Treatment of Depression in Adolescents and Young Adults." *Pediatrics* 138(6).

Moldad, O. 2017. March 31, 2017. "How Automated Interviews Drive Better Hiring Results." Vervoe, March 31. https://www.vervoe.com/blog/how-automated-interviews-drive-better-hiring-results.

Moltrecht, B., T. S. Davis, A. J. Shallcross, P. D. Visvanathan, and I. B. Mauss. 2014. "Mindfulness Versus Health Enhancement: How to Improve Emotion Regulation Among Those with a History of Nonsuicidal Self-Injury." Society for Personality and Social Psychology Emotion Pre-conference, Austin, TX.

Montage. 2014. "U.S. Job Seekers Impatient with Multiple Interview Rounds: Montage Study Finds Nearly Two Thirds of Active Job Seekers Think More Than Three Rounds of Interviews are Too Many." Montage. https://www.montagetalent.com/blog/kill-4th-interview-yes/.

Morse, S., and K. J Gergen. 1970. "Social Comparison, Self-Consistency, and the Concept of Self." *Journal of Personality and Social Psychology* 16 (1): 148.

Mulcahy, D. 2016. *The Gig Economy: The Complete Guide to Getting Better Work, Taking More Time Off, and Financing the Life You Want.* New York: AMACOM Books.

Neff, K. D., and C. K. Germer. 2013. "A Pilot Study and Randomized Controlled Trial of the Mindful Self-Compassion Program." *Journal of Clinical Psychology* 69 (1): 28–44. http://doi.org/10.1002/jclp.21923.

Nelson, S. K., M. D. Della Porta, K. J. Bao, H. C. Lee, I. Choi, and S. Lyubomirsky. 2015. "'It's Up to You': Experimentally Manipulated Autonomy Support for Prosocial Behavior Improves Well-Being in Two Cultures Over Six Weeks." *The Journal of Positive Psychology* 10 (5): 463–476.

Nolen-Hoeksema, S., and J. Morrow. 1991. "A Prospective Study of Depression and Posttraumatic Stress Symptoms after a Natural Disaster: The 1989 Loma Prieta Earthquake." *Journal of Personality and Social Psychology* 61 (1): 115–121.

Nook, E. C, D. C. Ong, S. A. Morelli, J. P. Mitchell, and J. Zaki. 2016. "Prosocial Conformity: Prosocial Norms Generalize Across Behavior and Empathy." *Personality and Social Psychology Bulletin* 42 (8): 1045–1062.

Panger, G. 2014. "Social Comparison in Social Media: A Look at Facebook and Twitter." CHI'14 Extended Abstracts on Human Factors in Computing Systems, Toronto, Ontario, April 26–May 1: 2095–2100.

Panger, G. T. 2017. "Emotion in Social Media." University of California, Berkeley.

Park, B. Y., G. Wilson, J. Berger, M. Christman, B. Reina, F. Bishop, W. P. Klam, and A. P. Doan. 2016. "Is Internet Pornography Causing Sexual Dysfunctions? A Review with Clinical Reports." *Behavioral Sciences* 6 (3): 17.

Posner, J., J. A. Russel, and B. S. Peterson. 2005. "The Circumplex Model of Affect: An Integrative Approach to Affective Neuroscience, Cognitive Development, and Psychopathology." *Development and Psychopathology* 17 (03): 715–734. http://doi.org/10.1017/S0954579405050340.

Przybylski, A. K., K. Murayama, C. R. DeHaan, and V. Gladwell. 2013. "Motivational, Emotional, and Behavioral Correlates of Fear of Missing Out." *Computers in Human Behavior* 29 (4): 1841–1848.

Przybylski, A. K., and N. Weinstein. 2013. "Can You Connect with Me Now? How the Presence of Mobile Communication Technology Influences Face-to-Face Conversation Quality." *Journal of Social and Personal Relationships* 30 (3): 237–246.

Quoidbach, J., E. V. Berry, M. Hansenne, and M. Mikolajczak. 2010. "Positive Emotion Regulation and Well-Being: Comparing the Impact of Eight Savoring and Dampening Strategies." *Personality and Individual Differences* 49 (5): 368–373.

Rainie, L., and K. Zickuhr. 2015. "Americans' Views on Mobile Etiquette." Pew Research Center, March 26. http://www.pewinternet.org/2015/08/26/americans-views-on-mobile-etiquette/.

Reis, H. T., K. M. Sheldon, S. L. Gable, J. Roscoe, and R. M. Ryan. 2000. "Daily Well-Being: The Role of Autonomy, Competence, and Relatedness." *Personality and Social Psychology Bulletin* 26 (4): 419–435.

Roberts, D. F., and U. G. Foehr. 2008. "Trends in Media Use." *The Future of Children* 18 (1): 11–37.

Royal Society of Public Health. 2017. "#StatusofMind." https://www.rsph.org.uk/our-work/campaigns/status-of-mind.html.

Ryan, R. M. , and E. L. Deci, E. L. and 2002. "Overview of Self-Determination Theory: An Organismic Dialectical Perspective." *Handbook of Self-Determination Research*: 3–33.

Sachs, J. D, R. Layard, and J. F. Helliwell. 2018. World Happiness Report 2018.

Sandstrom, G. M., and E. W. Dunn. 2014. "Is Efficiency Overrated? Minimal Social Interactions Lead to Belonging and Positive Affect." *Social Psychological and Personality Science* 5 (4): 437–442.

Schroeder, K. 2018. "In *Politics of Gross National Happiness*. New York: Springer.

Schutte, N., S. Toppinen, R. Kalimo, and W. Schaufeli. 2000. "The Factorial Validity of the Maslach Burnout Inventory—General Survey (MBI—GS) Across Occupational Groups and Nations." *Journal of Occupational and Organizational Psychology* 73 (1): 53–66.

Shallcross, A. J., J. J. Gross, P. D. Visvanathan, N. Kumar, A.Palfrey, B. Q. Ford, S. Dimidjian, S. Shirk, J. Holm-Denoma, K. M. Goode, E. Cox, W. Chaplin, and I. B. Mauss. 2015. "Relapse Prevention in Major Depressive Disorder: Mindfulness-Based Cognitive Therapy Versus an Active Control Condition." *Journal of Consulting and Clinical Psychology* 83 (5): 964–965.

Sheldon, K. M., and L. Houser-Marko. 2001. "Self-Concordance, Goal Attainment, and the Pursuit of Happiness: Can There Be an Upward Spiral?" *Journal of Personality and Social Psychology* 80 (1): 152–165.

Siegle, G. J., F. A. Ghinassi, and M. E. Thase. 2007. "Neurobehavioral Therapies in the 21st Century: Summary of an Emerging Field and an Extended Example of Cognitive Control Training for Depression." *Cognitive Therapy and Research* 31 (2): 235–262.

Smith, A. 2002. "Effects of Caffeine on Human Behavior." *Food and Chemical Toxicology* 40 (9): 1243–1255.

Soga, M., K. J. Gaston, and Y. Yamaura. 2017. "Gardening is Beneficial for Health: A Meta-Analysis." *Preventive Medicine Reports* 5: 92–99.

Steers, M. N., R. E. Wickham, and L. K. Acitelli. 2014. "Seeing Everyone Else's Highlight Reels: How Facebook Usage Is Linked to Depressive Symptoms." *Journal of Social and Clinical Psychology* 33 (8): 701–731.

Sullivan, J. 2014. "The Top 12 Reasons Why Slow Hiring Severely Damages Recruiting and Business Results."Ere Recruiting Intelligence, April 21. https://www.eremedia.com/ere/the-top-12-reasons-why-slow-hiring -severely-damages-recruiting-and-business-results/.

Sun, C., A. Bridges, J. A. Johnson, and M. B. Ezzell. 2016. "Pornography and the Male Sexual Script: An Analysis of Consumption and Sexual Relations." *Archives of Sexual Behavior* 45 (4): 983–994.

Tajfel, H. 1970. "Experiments in Intergroup Discrimination." *Scientific American* 223 (5): 96–103.

Tajfel, H. 1982. "Social Psychology of Intergroup Relations." *Annual Review of Psychology* 33 (1): 1–39.

Tamir, M., O. P. John, S. Srivastava, and J. J. Gross. 2007. "Implicit Theories of Emotion: Affective and Social Outcomes Across a Major Life Transition." *Journal of Personality and Social Psychology* 92 (4): 731–744. http://doi.org/10.1037/0022-3514.92.4.731.

Tandoc, E. C., P. Ferrucci, and M. Duffy. 2015. "Facebook Use, Envy, and Depression Among College Students: Is Facebooking Depressing?" *Computers in Human Behavior* 43: 139–146.

Tromholt, M. 2016. "The Facebook Experiment: Quitting Facebook Leads to Higher Levels of Well-Being." *Cyberpsychology, Behavior, and Social Networking* 19 (11): 661–666.

Troy, A. S., F. H. Wilhelm, A. J. Shallcross, and I. B. Mauss. 2010. "Seeing the Silver Lining: Cognitive Reappraisal Ability Moderates the Relationship Between Stress and Depressive Symptoms." *Emotion* 10 (6): 783–795. http://doi.org/10.1037/a0020262.

Twenge, J. M. 2000. "The Age of Anxiety? The Birth Cohort Change in Anxiety and Neuroticism, 1952–1993." *Journal of Personality and Social Psychology* 79 (6): 1007.

Twenge, J. M. 2015. "Time Period and Birth Cohort Differences in Depressive Symptoms in the US, 1982–2013." *Social Indicators Research* 121 (2): 437–454.

Twenge, J. M., T. E. Joiner, M. L. Rogers, and G. N. Martin. 2018. "Increases in Depressive Symptoms, Suicide-Related Outcomes, and Suicide Rates Among U.S. Adolescents after 2010 and Links to Increased New Media Screen Time." *Clinical Psychological Science* 6 (1): 3–17.

Van Deursen, A. J. A. M., C. L. Bolle, S. M. Hegner, and P. A. M. Kommers. 2015. "Modeling Habitual and Addictive Smartphone Behavior: The Role of Smartphone Usage Types, Emotional Intelligence, Social Stress, Self-Regulation, Age, and Gender." *Computers in Human Behavior* 45: 411–420.

Verduyn, P., O. Ybarra, M. Résibois, J. Jonides, and E. Kross. 2017. "Do Social Network Sites Enhance or Undermine Subjective Well-Being? A Critical Review." *Social Issues and Policy Review* 11 (1): 274–302.

Wadlinger, H. A., and D. M. Isaacowitz. 2008. "Looking Happy: The Experimental Manipulation of a Positive Visual Attention Bias." *Emotion* 8 (1): 121–126.

Walsh, R. 2011. "Lifestyle and Mental Health." *American Psychologist* 66 (7): 579.

Tchiki Davis, PhD, is a technology consultant, writer of the blog *Click Here for Happiness* for *Psychology Today,* and cocreator of online programs that have helped more than a million people worldwide find balance and joy.

Foreword writer **Melanie Greenberg, PhD,** is a practicing clinical and health psychologist in Marin County, CA; a top social media influencer in her field; and writer of the blog *The Mindful Self-Express* for *Psychology Today.*

Register your **new harbinger** titles for additional benefits!

When you register your **new harbinger** title—purchased in any format, from any source—you get access to benefits like the following:

- Downloadable accessories like printable worksheets and extra content

- Instructional videos and audio files

- Information about updates, corrections, and new editions

Not every title has accessories, but we're adding new material all the time.

Access free accessories in 3 easy steps:

1. Sign in at NewHarbinger.com (or **register** to create an account).

2. Click on **register a book**. Search for your title and click the **register** button when it appears.

3. Click on the **book cover or title** to go to its details page. Click on **accessories** to view and access files.

That's all there is to it!

If you need help, visit:

NewHarbinger.com/accessories

new harbinger
CELEBRATING
40 YEARS